A 60-Minute Guide to Microcomputers

Lew Hollerbach

A SPECTRUM BOOK

Prentice-Hall, Inc., Englewood Cliffs, N.J. 07632

Library of Congress Cataloging in Publication Data

HOLLERBACH, LEW.
A 60-minute guide to microcomputers.

A Spectrum Book.
Includes index.
1. Microcomputers. I. Title. II. Title: Sixty-minute guide to microcomputers.
QA76.5.H635 1982 001.64 82-12232
ISBN 0-13-811430-7

This book is available at a special discount when ordered in large quantities. Contact Prentice-Hall, Inc., General Publishing Division, Special Sales, Englewood Cliffs, N.J. 07632.

Cover design by Jeanette Jacobs
Cover illustration by Jim Kinstrey
Editorial/production supervision and interior design by Suse L. Cioffi
Manufacturing buyer: Barbara Frick

A SPECTRUM BOOK.

ISBN 0-13-811430-7

ISBN 0-13-811422-6 {PBK.}

10 9 8 7 6 5 4 3

Printed in the United States of America

Originally published as *Computer Crunch: At Home with Computers* by The Orlando Press, Bath, England. © 1981 Lew Hollerbach and Orlando Language Texts Ltd.

PRENTICE HALL INTERNATIONAL, INC., *London*
PRENTICE-HALL OF AUSTRALIA PTY. LIMITED, *Sydney*
PRENTICE-HALL OF CANADA INC., *Toronto*
PRENTICE-HALL OF INDIA PRIVATE LIMITED, *New Delhi*
PRENTICE-HALL OF JAPAN, INC., *Tokyo*
PRENTICE-HALL OF SOUTHEAST ASIA PTE. LTD., *Singapore*
WHITEHALL BOOKS LIMITED, *Wellington, New Zealand*

CONTENTS

1
Introducing Computers
1

2
The Processor
6

3
The Program
17

4
Input and Output
28

5
Types of Hardware and Software
69

6
Analyzing the Needs
78

7
Recognizing the Solutions
81

8
Evaluating Systems
88

9
Implementation
101

Glossaries
113

Index
133

1
INTRODUCING COMPUTERS

THE USE AND USEFULNESS OF A COMPUTER

What is a computer? It is a machine, and like any other machine, it does useful work for you, providing you give it some guidance, or control it. The most important difference between a computer and other machines is that the computer is not fixed to any single task—it is an adaptable machine.

The computer can perform almost any task that can be divided into a number of procedures, and expressed in terms of a series of instructions. The computer can be made to do tasks by giving it the instructions for those tasks. Without these instructions, a computer can do nothing.

The distinguishing features of a computer are:

- it consists entirely of electronic circuitry, and has no moving parts;
- it is very much faster than any mechanical machine, and more reliable;
- it is very compact, considering the amount of work it can do and the speed at which it does it.

Computers and Software Packages

Memory	*Games and Recreational Software*	*Education*	*Housekeeping*	*Professional*
	simulations, board games, arcade games	number skills, remedial sciences, languages, self-improvement	filing systems, simple accounts, check book balance, word processors	accounts, financial information, databases, word processors, scientific applications, modelling and decision tools, specialized packages for lawyers, doctors, dentists etc. Link up with view data stock markets, general communications
5–8K	✓	✓		
16K	✓	✓	✓	
32K	✓	✓	✓ word processing	
48–64K	✓ more sophisticated simulations such as flying	✓	✓	✓ tailor-made programs word processing
128K	✓	✓	✓	✓

The same can be said of many electronic machines: What makes the computer unique?

- The computer carries out only a few very simple operations.
- A task must always be made up of the computer's operations.
- The computer will do the task by carrying out the instructions making up that task.
- For a computer to do a different task, all it needs is a different set of instructions.
- A computer carries out its operations at very high speed.

Why are computers used? The reasons for the computer's widespread use are its versatility, speed, compactness, and cost-effectiveness for many applications. Computers are used because:

- some tasks could take people an excessively long time to do;
- some tasks are so repetitive that human resources are wasted;
- some tasks cannot be physically performed by people, or are too hazardous for people.

The word *computer* is in many ways a misnomer, since computers are not solely for computational tasks. The name has stayed because the first computers were used for calculations. What computers are now used for, is:

- **Number crunching.** Performing the basic arithmetic operations on numbers. The benefit of using computers is speed—very large quantities of numbers can be operated on in a small time, without error.

Applications range from simple bookkeeping sums to complex scientific calculations.

- **Text processing.** Working with letters, words, and paragraphs instead of numbers. A primary benefit is speed, but the facilities for changing, or rearranging, text are unique to these machines.
- **Measurement and control.** Computers can be used to measure physical entities, such as pressure or temperature, and to control the operation of other devices, such as motors or valves. In such cases, the computer is an extension of the human senses.

Common to all applications is the need to store numbers, letters, or information about physical entities, and computers can also do this in a highly organized yet compact way.

What can't computers do? They can't:

- create as people can. Like any tool, computers have no facility to originate—they can only work under the guidance of their operators.

THE LANGUAGE OF COMPUTERS

To appreciate the use and usefulness of computers, you must have an understanding of what they do and how they work. You must know the language in which the relevant information is expressed. Most of this language is jargon:

- many words are familiar, because the concepts behind them have parallels in noncomputer areas;
- many of the words are commonly used ones, but have taken on a new meaning;

- many words are artificial, created by leading companies in the computer industry, like IBM;
- there are many abbreviations and acronyms (words formed from the first letter, or first few letters, of several other words). Abbreviations and acronyms are useful—they can be used as a form of shorthand in writing and speaking.

Jargon words aren't a problem once you get used to them. To help you, there are a few dictionaries published. There are problems, however:

- some of the abbreviations have become words—*i.e.*, the letters are not spoken individually, but as a word;
- often, the abbreviations and acronyms are written as words (normally, they would be written in capitals).

2
THE PROCESSOR

INTRODUCTION

There are two sides to the computer—the machine itself, and the instructions that make it work. Consider first the machine.

For the computer to be useful, you must give it something to do.

- Anything that goes into the computer is called **input**.

Once the computer has done its work, it gives you the results of its work.

- Anything that comes out of the computer is called **output**.

The work that a computer does is called a **process**.

> *Note*: These three terms may also be used as verbs; hence something is input for processing, and the results are output.

DATA AND INFORMATION

What is put in? What comes out? What is being processed? Data and information are two familiar words, often used interchangeably, but there is a difference:

- **Data:** a representation of something; the basic facts that can be processed; *e.g.*, the number 6.
- **Information:** data arranged to be meaningful to you; *i.e.*, data put in some sort of context; *e.g.*, *6 apples*.

Data is what is being input, output, and processed, and this is why using a computer is called **data processing (DP)**. Data processing is the useful work done by the computer.

How is data processed?

- The computer is an electronic machine, so electrical **signals** are used.
- Signals are physical conveyors of data.
- The data is conveyed by two types, or levels, of signal, because it is very easy to manipulate signals that only have two levels.

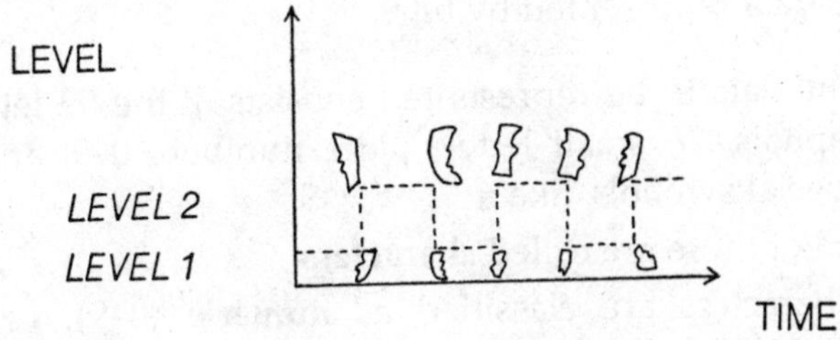

- Manipulation in this case simply means changing the level of the signal.

- Since there are only two levels, this representation of data is called **binary** (binary = 2).
- Each level can be symbolized by a digit, and since there are two levels, there can be two digits, and hence each digit is called a **binary digit**.
- Because computers use these digits, they are called **digital** machines.
- A binary digit is called a **bit** (**b**inary dig**it**).
- A bit is the fundamental unit of data, and any data can be reduced to bits.

Processing is the manipulation of bits, according to a predefined procedure.

- Data must be reduced to bits, or a pattern of bits, so that each piece of data has its own unique pattern.
- A collection or pattern of bits is called a **byte** (this is an artificial word).
- A typical size of byte is 8 (*i.e.*, 8 bits make up one byte), since there can be enough permutations of 8 bits to represent all the data.
- A byte is a number consisting of 8 binary digits.

How is data represented by bits?

- The data to be represented consists of the 52 letters (26 capitals, 26 small letters), the numbers 0–9, and some special symbols, like + , . * : – $.
- All of these are called **characters.**
- Characters are classified as **numeric** (0–9), or **alphanumeric** (letters, symbols, and numbers).
- By international agreement, a unique pattern of 8 bits has been assigned to each character.
- This unique pattern is called the **ASCII** code (pronounced 'askee').

- ACSII is the **A**merican **S**tandard **C**ode of **I**nformation **I**nterchange, and it is used universally in almost all computers.

The computer must perform these actions when processing data:

- input the characters making up the data;
- convert each character to bits;
- manipulate the bits as needed (for example adding numbers;
- decode the new bit patterns into characters, and new data.

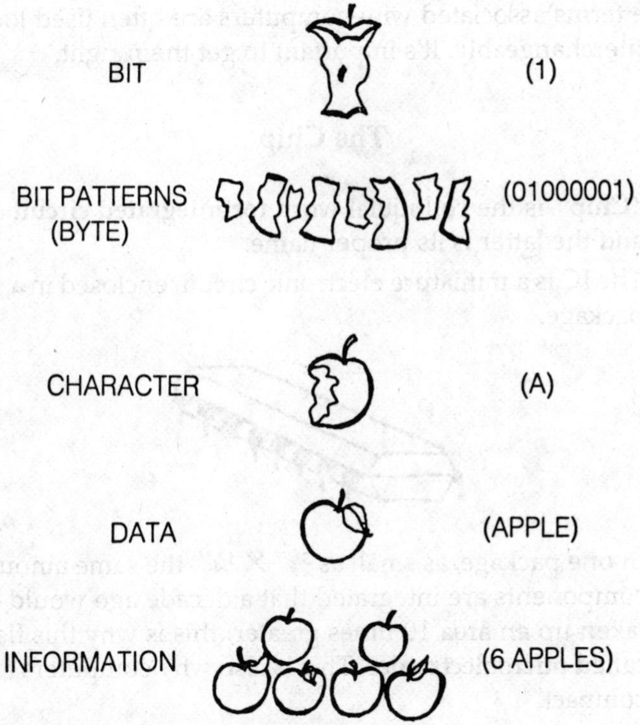

The power of computers is simply the ability to manipulate bits at extremely high speed.

To summarize, the hierarchy of data is as follows, from lowest to highest level:

- bits;
- bit patterns (bytes);
- characters;
- data;
- information.

BUILDING BLOCKS OF A COMPUTER

Three terms associated with computers are often used loosely and interchangeably. It's important to get them right.

The Chip

- **"Chip"** is the colloquial word for **integrated circuit (IC)**, and the latter is its proper name.
- The IC is a miniature electronic circuit, enclosed in a small package.

- In one package, as small as ¾″ × ¼″, the same amount of components are integrated that a decade ago would have taken up an area 10 times greater; this is why this field is called **microelectronics**. This is also why computers are so compact.

- The chip got its name because the electronic circuitry is chipped off a large master **wafer**, and then enclosed in a plastic package.

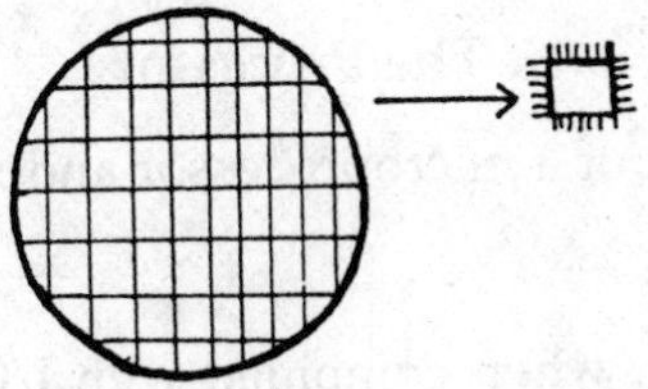

- The IC does work on electrical signals—modifying their levels, timing and other properties.

The Microprocessor

- A **microprocessor** is an IC, but quite a large one. It is the equivalent of many ICs in one package.
- A microprocessor contains all the components needed to perform the basic data processing functions.

The microprocessor provides the basic building block of a computer. It reduces the number of separate components needed. As a result:

- cost is decreased since fewer components are used;
- speed is increased, since the electrical signals have a shorter distance to travel.

A microprocessor is not a computer:

- A microprocessor cannot do anything on its own: it must be connected to other components.
- These components are the memory, a power supply, and devices that get data in and out of the processor and memory.

- Devices that get data into and out of the processor are called **I/O** (**I**nput/**O**utput) devices (keyboard, printer etc.).

The Processor

The combination of a microprocessor and memory is called a **processor**.

- A processor, when combined with I/O devices, forms a computer. The word *computer* is a collective noun used to describe the working group of processor, memory, and I/O devices.
- A computer is a **system**, and the generic term for the components is **hardware**. A system is a group of separate components, connected together to function as a unit (keyboard, microprocessors, VDU, etc.).
- The processor and memory are contained in one case and the I/O devices in another. For this reason, I/O devices are called **peripherals**.

THE NEED FOR MEMORY

Consider a situation where a lot of numbers have to be added up:

- they will be written down, since it's unlikely that a person could remember them all;
- writing these numbers on paper can be regarded as a form of temporary storage.

The processor also needs to store its instructions, and any data that it will need. This storage is called **memory**.

- Memory consists of chips, and each chip can store a certain number of bits.
- Storage in this sense is holding a signal at its current level.
- The unit of measurement of the size of the memory is the byte, or more conveniently, the **Kilobyte.**
- A Kilobyte (**K**) is not 1000 bytes, but 1024 bytes. Hence, 8K = 8196 bytes of storage. (Often, **Kb** is also used as an abbreviation for Kilobyte.)
- The number of bytes stored in a chip depends on how many bits in the byte, and how many bits the chip can store.
- The more memory you have, the more instructions and data you can store.

In practice, there is a limit to the amount of memory you can have, and this depends on:

- the internal construction of the microprocessor (this is called its **architecture**).

All processors need some memory to do their useful work, and the amount depends on the application. For example:

- a washing machine may use a microprocessor, using a small amount of memory, say 2K;
- a typical small computer may have a lot more memory, say 64K.

TYPES OF MEMORIES

You will come across two types of memories used with processors: **RAM** and **ROM**.

RAM

- **RAM** (pronounced ram) is an abbreviation for **Random Access Memory**; this is a misnomer, but has come into widespread use. It really should be RWM, for Read/Write Memory (it is easier to say 'ram' than 'rwm').
- RAM can have data stored in it, and extracted from it; *i.e.*, it can be written to, and read from (hence read/write).
- RAM can have its contents altered—new data can be stored, overwriting what was previously there.
- RAM is **volatile**—it loses its contents when power is turned off from the computer.

ROM

- **ROM** is an abbreviation for **Read-Only Memory**.
- ROM can have its contents read, but data cannot be written to it, except once, during its manufacture.
- ROM is nonvolatile—when power is off, it doesn't lose its contents.
- ROM cannot have its contents altered; once data is stored there, it stays there.

How are these memories used?

- ROM is used to store data that will never change, and you never have direct access to this data.
- RAM stores variable data, which you can access; as a rule, your computer will have more RAM than ROM.

Finally, note the following:

- almost every computer will use both types of memory;
- both memories are random-access, *i.e.*, any part of memory can be accessed in the same time;

- the consequence of random-access is very high speed; the time taken to get a bit out of memory can be as little as a few ten-millionths of a second.

There are two more memory types you may come across: **PROM** and **EPROM.**

PROM

- **PROM** (pronounced 'prom') is a **Programmable Read-Only Memory.**
- The difference between PROM and ROM is that you can program a PROM; ROMs can only be programmed where and when they are made.
- Nevertheless, you can only store data in it once; it behaves just like a ROM otherwise.

EPROM

- **EPROM** is an **Erasable PROM**; it offers the same facility as a PROM, but its contents can change.
- The difference between EPROM and RAM is that EPROM is nonvolatile.
- EPROMs can be erased with ultraviolet light.

PROMs and EPROMs are used mainly for development and prototyping, in special applications.

CHARACTERISTICS OF PROCESSORS

When investigating different types of processors, you'll come across some broad specifications used to describe them; these are:

- Designation of microprocessor(s) used; this is usually a number, or letter/number combination, such as 8086, 6809, Z8000.
- Word size: not always given directly, but can be deduced sometimes from the designation; it refers to the number of bits used in the microprocessor's byte. Typical values are 8 and 16.
- Capacity: the amount of memory that can be accessed, both RAM and ROM. The word size has some bearing on this.
- Processor speed: measured in Megahertz (a unit of frequency); the higher the frequency, the faster it is.

Remember that these characteristics apply to the processor only: there will be more quoted for the whole computer, such as:

- languages, available software, interfaces, and peripherals.

3
THE PROGRAM

INSTRUCTIONS

The popularity of the computer as an all-purpose machine is due to:

- its ability to carry out a few basic operations at very high speed;
- its ability to perform different jobs, given only different sets of instructions.

To make a computer do a job, you must give it instructions, and these instructions must be expressed in terms of the basic operations that the processor can carry out.

The set of instructions that the processor can use to do a job is called a **program**.

The generic name given to computer programs is software. It is "soft" because:

- programs are stored in memory as electrical signals—you can't see or feel them;

- you can only have indirect experience of programs, by their effects or consequences.

COMPUTER LANGUAGE

To give a processor instructions, you must first have a means of expressing these instructions, and secondly be able to communicate them to the processor.

Languages are used by people to communicate with one another. These languages are called natural languages. How do people communicate with computers? They use artificial, computer languages.

There are differences between these languages.

Natural Languages

- Grow and become established by natural evolution.
- Are used to communicate a large variety of information.
- Have complex syntax (grammatical rules).
- Have expressions which can be ambiguous.
- Use a large vocabulary.

Artificial Languages

- Are designed and constructed—there is no natural evolution.
- Communicate a small amount of information.
- Have simple syntax, use a small vocabulary, and are free of ambiguities.

Computer programs are written in artificial computer languages. These languages:

- have as elements verbs and subjects, just as natural languages.

The instructions, which make up the program:

- each consist of statements. These are the elements (see below) arranged according to the syntax of the language.

If you were writing a program, you would be listing the statements, one after the other, in the order necessary to perform the task you need. The processor will act on these instructions, in the same order and in sequence—the instructions are processed one after the other.

What are these elements? There are only a very few element types in a computer language. The main ones are:

- **input/output:** these get data in and out of the processor;
- **arithmetic:** these perform the basic arithmetic operations;
- **decision-making:** the program can make comparisons between different data, and make decisions according to the outcome.

You've seen that the processor can only work with bits. How are the computer languages used?

- Each model of microprocessor has its own instruction set. Different manufacturers have different instruction sets, although they are quite similar.
- The instruction set is a collection of instructions, which have been built into the microprocessor during its manufacture.
- The instructions, like all data, are made up of bit patterns.

To have the processor do work, you must:

- have a program, consisting of instructions from the microprocessor's instruction set;
- have the processor "read" these instructions.

Once the processor encounters an instruction, it compares it to its repertoire; if it finds a match, it will act on it.

This is the way computers work in practice:

- Via some input device, a program is entered, and stored in RAM.
- The processor starts the program (the instructions are read and acted on).
- Data is input, processed, and output, according to the program for the job being done, until the last instruction is reached.
- The processor stops, at which stage another program can be entered.

LEVELS OF LANGUAGES

The microprocessor's native language, its instruction set, is called **machine code**. Code in this context has its normal meaning: it is a set of letters or digits which are arbitrarily assigned a meaning or action.

- Writing programs in machine code is tedious and error-prone, since every instruction has to be expressed as a bit pattern.
- To overcome this difficulty, languages were developed that used three- or four-letter acronyms, called **mnemonics**, to symbolize each machine code instruction.
- Instead of writing bit patterns, English letters are used.

- Each mnemonic corresponds to one machine code instruction.

Assembler, or **Assembly language**, is the name given to a language that uses mnemonics to symbolize machine code.

Assembler is categorized as a low-level language.

- A **low-level language** is one which is "close" to the microprocessor's native language.
- This means it does not resemble English, or any other human language.

Writing programs in a low-level language can also be tedious and error-prone, so languages were further developed to use English or Englishlike statements, rather than mnemonics.

Languages that are "closer" to the way people communicate are called high-level languages. This is the way a high-level language works:

- A **high-level language** is a program that is supplied by the manufacturer of the processor.
- It has as its input English or Englishlike statements.
- It checks the syntax of each statement, and if correct, generates the equivalent machine code instructions for that statement.
- English is the standard language usec for expressing high-level computer language statements.

There are two commonly used ways of translating high-level statements to machine code: the statements may be interpreted or compiled, and hence the high-level languages are called **interpreters** or **compilers**.

Interpreters

- An **interpreter** takes one statement at a time and translates it into machine code.
- It works in the same way as a human interpreter, translating one statement at a time from one language to another.
- If you have to use the program again, the statements have to be translated anew; *i.e.*, the machine code equivalents are not preserved, and have to be created each time the program is used.
- Interpreting is not a very efficient way of using programs.
- Interpreters are used because the people who write programs find them easy to use.

Compilers

- A **compiler** takes all the statements and translates them into machine code. It does this once—the translation does not have to be done each time the program is to be used.
- This is equivalent to translating a whole book from cover to cover before reading it. Compare this to translating one sentence at a time, using an interpreter.
- Compiling is more efficient than interpreting, although not as easy to use.
- A program works faster if it is written in a compiled language rather than in an interpreted language.

You will come across two terms when describing compiled programs:

- **source program:** this is the program consisting of high-level statements—it has not yet been translated;
- **object program:** this is the machine code equivalent of the source program—it has been translated.

To summarize, given that a program can be written in both a

low-level and high-level language, there are two disadvantages to using the high-level language:

- The speed of the program is reduced; in most cases, a low-level program works faster than even a compiled program. This is because more machine code is generated for high-level statements.
- Since there are more instructions, more memory is used.

In most cases, none of these poses a problem. Only in the cases where speed and memory are at a premium should low-level languages be considered.

All processors have facilities for writing programs in their low-level language. The choice of high-level languages offered depends on the processor manufacturer, and also on whether other companies, that specialize only in writing languages for specific makes of machines, offer languages.

Finally, how much room in memory do programs take up?

- On most of the small computers available at the moment, each microprocessor instruction takes up either two or three bytes of memory.

Hence, in a 48K memory (49152 bytes), you could hold a low-level program about 15000 instructions long.

- In a typical interpreted language, this would be equivalent to about 2000 high-level instructions.

APPLICATION OF LANGUAGES—SOME EXAMPLES

Consider three areas of application of computers together with the languages that are used, and the reason for their use: these areas are commerce, science, and education.

Commerce

- The main uses of computers in commerce are for storing and retrieving information.
- Data storage requirements comprise high-speed storage and retrieval, and facility to change selected parts of the data without affecting other parts.
- There is little emphasis on complex calculations.

COBOL is a popular commercial language. Its full name is **CO**mmon **B**usiness-**O**riented **L**anguage.

- It makes it easy to express the data storage requirements for a commercial application.
- It was designed to be self-documenting: *i.e.*, you didn't need to be a computer expert to understand what was being done in the program; however, this hasn't proved successful.

Science

Scientific work is heavily involved with calculations.

- At one extreme, there may be a few simple formulae, but many variables change, and it is necessary to recalculate for every change. Statistical calculations are an example.
- The other extreme is many very complex equations that have to be solved quickly, such as those for designing a building.

FORTRAN is another popular language, but for scientific and engineering uses. It has little use in commercial applications. FORTRAN is an acronym for **FOR**mula **TRAN**slation.

- It allows scientists and engineers to translate their formulae into high-level language statements very easily, without learning too much about the syntax of the language.
- It also provides all the mathematical functions—such as trigonometric and algebraic—that are needed for such work.

Education

Languages in this area must fulfil two requirements:

- They must be easy to assimilate and implement by educators without the educators being computer experts.
- If used by students, they must enable the student to learn the correct programming techniques.

Consider the first requirement:

- **PILOT** is a language developed by educators—it is easy to use, but provides many facilities for designing **courseware** (computer-based teaching materials).
- **Pascal** is widely used for teaching students programming and elements of computer science. Its feature is the ease with which solutions to problems can be expressed, and it also forces the student into good programming habits.

  Note: Pascal is not an acronym—it is named after a French mathematician.

One popular language is **BASIC**. It is used for teaching, commercial, and some scientific work.

- It is easy to learn and easy to use, and is found on almost all the small computers.
- BASIC stands for **B**eginner's **A**ll-purpose **S**ymbolic **I**nstruction **C**ode.

Most computer languages are designed by computer scientists and committees, and adhere to standards set down by **ANSI**—the **American National Standards Institute**.

Pascal, FORTRAN, and COBOL are examples of compiled languages, whereas BASIC is an interpreted language.

These are just a few of the very many computer languages being used. Some are in widespread use, others have a very limited application. Many processor manufacturers also design their own languages, which can only be used on their machines.

PROGRAMMING

As with natural languages, certain styles and techniques are used when writing in computer languages. In theory, as long as the program performs its function correctly, it doesn't matter how it does it. In practice, this is not so, programs are written to:

- perform their task at maximum speed;
- conserve resources, such as memory;
- give maximum benefit to the user, and be easy to use.

Programs written in such a way are elegant—they are efficient. To write such programs requires a knowledge of:

- the computer, and its characteristics;
- the application being programmed;
- certain generally-accepted procedures for performing a given task, and those specific to the task.

These procedures are called **algorithms**—they lay down the rules of logic necessary to perform the task.

The art and science of writing programs is called programming. Whether programming is easy or not is a contentious issue:

- Programming is easy, since the vocabulary of a computer language is small and easy to learn.
- Programming is not easy, since to write elegant programs, the techniques and methods to use require more than a knowledge of the language's vocabulary.

Computer programmers are classed as professionals, and hence they must have training and experience. For personal use, such discipline is not required, since the main aims are "power over the machine," and simple programming. For more sophisticated work, knowledge of algorithms becomes important.

4
INPUT AND OUTPUT

INTERFACES

To use a processor to advantage, it must be connected to peripherals. What is a peripheral, and why is it so called?

- It is a device that converts binary data into a form that can be assimilated by humans, or perhaps by other, non-computer, devices.
- A processor can only process data. There must be means of getting data into the processor, and also for seeing or recording the results of processing.
- Devices that get data into and out of the processor are called **peripherals.** Peripherals are so called because they are not part of the processor. Nevertheless, you can't use a processor without them. All I/O devices are peripherals.

The connection between a processor and a peripheral is accomplished using an **interface.**

The interface determines what I/O device is connected to the processor. You can connect to a processor devices that:

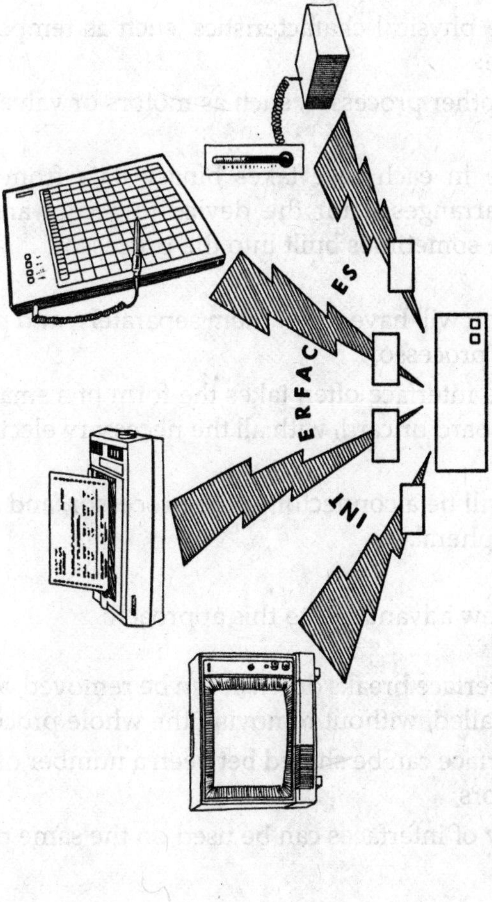
INTERFACES

- convert binary data to words and numbers, and print them on paper;
- store binary data on to more permanent storage media;
- produce precision drawings;
- measure physical characteristics, such as temperature or pressure;
- control other processes, such as motors or valves.

The interface in each case takes binary data from the processor, and arranges it for the device to accept and act on. Interfaces are sometimes built into the processor.

- If not, you will have to get them separately, and plug them into the processor.
- If so, the interface often takes the form of a small printed circuit board or card, with all the necessary electronics on it.
- There will be a connector to the processor, and a cable to the peripheral.

There are a few advantages to this approach:

- if the interface breaks down, it can be removed, and a new one installed, without removing the whole processor;
- the interface can be shared between a number of identical processors;
- a variety of interfaces can be used on the same processor.

Standards

Interfaces have been standardized to a large extent, so that various types of equipment from different manufacturers can be used together.

All the manufacturer has to do is ensure his equipment conforms to the standard. The standards define:

- the way the data is transmitted and received;
- the signal types and levels;
- the way the sockets, plugs, and wires are interconnected.

Each standard was devised by a governing body, and is usually known by a name and number. Each body has set standards for many applications of data transmission, not only for computers.

Two standards you'll come across frequently are:

- **EIA**—**E**lectronics **I**nstitute of **A**merica. Interface: EIA RS232
- **IEEE**—**I**nstitute of **E**lectrical and **E**lectronic **E**ngineers. Interface: IEEE 488.

Some manufacturers of processors do not adhere to any of the international standards—they have their own. An example is IBM. Often, their processors may have certain special features or facilities, which you may need to use, but if you haven't got their equipment, you can't do so. You may find that some peripherals, such as VDUs, have **emulators**.

- Emulators are built into the peripheral—they are not a separate attachment.
- Emulators are in effect translators: They convert data presentation, as defined by one of the international standards, into the presentation of a specific manufacturer, or vice versa.
- Some manufacturers build equipment to be specifically compatible with a certain other make. These manufacturers are called **Plug-Compatible Manufacturers (PCM)**, since their equipment plugs in to other equipment.

Types of Interfaces

There are two widely used interfaces: **serial** and **parallel**.

Serial Interfaces

- Enable data to flow as a sequence of bits, one after the other (rather like a line of people walking in and out of a door).
- Are technically simpler than parallel interfaces; they are slightly cheaper, and slightly more versatile.
- Allow operation of peripherals at a distance.

A common serial interface for many computer peripherals is the **RS232 (V24)**.

Parallel Interfaces

- Enable data to flow with bits parallel to each other, at the same time (like a multi-lane motorway with the cars all going in the same direction).
- Are faster in operation than serial.
- Have no fixed standard—they are usually specific to manufacturers.

One common parallel interface is the **Centronics** interface, named after the company which first started making them.

You may come across a parallel interface designated the **IEEE 488**. It is also called the **General Purpose Interface Bus (GPIB)**.

The GPIB:

- has been specifically developed for interfacing scientific and control equipment to processors;
- is a versatile and high-speed interface, but quite expensive and complex.

The term **bus** refers to a path along which data flows from one of many sources to one of many destinations. The path is a series of contiguous wires.

In the strict sense, the definition applies only to the interconnection of the microprocessor and memory.

The term is sometimes also used when describing the interconnection of the processor and peripherals. If so, you'll come across the **S50** and **S100** buses.

S50 and S100 are 50-wire and 100-wire buses, respectively.

The type of interface you get depends on:

- what types are available for your processor;
- what type is needed for a given peripheral;
- what application is envisaged.

Sometimes you won't have to worry about getting interfaces—one or more come built into the processor.

If this is the case, you'll see the processor manufacturer quoting the number and types of **ports** the machine has.

- A port in a processor is like an air or seaport: traffic comes into it, and comes out of it. The traffic in this case is data—the port is an entrance and exit for data.
- The more ports a processor has, the more peripherals can be connected to it. The advantage of this is greater flexibility.

Transmission

Transmission is:

- the reproduction of source data at a particular destination. For example, data is transmitted from the processor (source) to a peripheral (destination).

There are a few parameters that govern the transmission of data. These are often quoted in literature on processors or peripherals. They are very technical in nature, and all you have to do with them is to make sure that both the processor and peripheral are set to the same values.

Transmission speed is an example—the peripheral must receive data at the same rate that the processor transmits it; this is like tuning your radio to a transmitter's frequency.

- Most times the processor will determine what the values for the parameters are.
- The peripheral will often have a set of switches, which you can set so as to correspond with the processor's values.

Timing

During transmission, the processor and peripheral must *know* what the other is doing; *i.e.*, they must be coordinated. This means that the processor and peripheral keep in step with respect to time when data is being transmitted—this is called synchronization. Two ways of transmitting are:

- **Synchronous transmission:** processor and peripheral are kept in step continuously by one timing mechanism in the processor. The processor sets the timing, the peripheral obeys it, and this mechanism is always in effect.
- **Asynchronous transmission:** processor and peripheral are not kept in step continously. In asynchronous transmission, each chunk of data, say a byte of 8 bits, has **start bits** in front of it. As soon as a peripheral intercepts these start bits, it switches on its own timing mechanism, and timing is kept for the length of transmission. At the end of the data, **stop bits** are encountered, and timing switches off.

What method is used depends on the equipment, what medium is used (telephone lines, etc.) and the application. You don't need to decide the method, as this is determined by the manufacturers.

Modes

It's usual for the peripheral to transmit some data to the processor. This data may inform the processor whether:

- the peripheral is ready to accept data from the processor—it sends a READY signal;
- the peripheral is busy and cannot accept any data—it sends a BUSY signal;
- an error has occurred, such as a printer running out of paper—it sends an ERROR signal.

Transmission modes are described as:

- **Simplex:** you won't find this too often—it means transmission of data in one direction only.
- **Half-Duplex (HDX):** data flows in both directions (*i.e.*, to and from the peripheral or processor), but only in one direction at a time.
- **Full-Duplex,** also **Duplex (FDX):** data flows in both directions, and at the same time.

Error Checking

Data must be checked to ensure it hasn't been modified during transmission. **Parity** is one of the ways of doing this checking.

- Parity is the addition of a bit to the data being transmitted, and then adding all the bits up, seeing whether the sum is odd or even.

Once the data has been received, the same calculation is performed, and the results compared:

> **odd parity:** the sum is odd;
>
> **even parity:** the sum is even;
>
> **no parity:** no parity is used.

The parity bit is not part of the data—you don't see it or have access to it. All the calculations are done internally, by the hardware. Parity is only one of many means used to ensure integrity in the transmission of data.

Speeds

- **Baud rate:** this is the unit of measurement of speed of transmission, expressed in bits per second, but only for serial data transmission. Typical values are: 50, 110, 150, 300, 600, 1200, 1800, 2000, 2400, 4800, 7200, 9600, 19200.

To summarize, the interface makes input and output (I/O) possible; it:

- arranges data so it is compatible between processor and peripheral;
- controls transmission of data to and from the peripheral;
- ensures faithful reproduction at the destination, by checking for transmission errors.

VDU AND KEYBOARDS

Visual Display Units

The **Visual Display Unit (VDU)** is the most common and convenient way to enter data into the processor. The term is generally applied to the combination of screen and keyboard.

The screen consists of a **Cathode Ray Tube (CRT)**, and is technically the same as a television screen. It may be monochrome (black and white, or green), color, or have a combination of tints.

The **keyboard** is a collection of switches, each one representing a character, as in a typewriter keyboard. When a key is pressed, a character is generated, and displayed on the screen.

Why is a VDU so common and so convenient? Consider some of its features:

- It is easy to enter data with a keyboard—all you do is press the required keys. This is why entering data is sometimes called **keying.**
- As you press a key, the corresponding character is displayed on the screen; you can always see what you are keying.
- Mistakes in keying are easy to correct. Only when you are completely sure that everything is correct do you send it to the processor.

- The processor can communicate with you via the screen—you can be asked for data, or you can be sent data, or you can receive messages.
- The screen is silent and very fast in operation. It is easy to clear it and display new data, as often as needed; there is no noise, and no resources—such as paper—are wasted.
- It is a reliable device—the only moving parts are the key switches. If treated properly, a VDU lasts a very long time.

Remember that the VDU is a two-way device: you can see what you are sending to the processor, and also what is being sent to you.

You may have no choice in the type of VDU you get when you buy a system. It may be:

- built into the processor;
- a separate TV-like monitor, with the keyboard integrated with the processor;
- a **standalone** VDU, where the keyboard and screen are in one enclosure, separate from the processor (*standalone* means self-contained).

A **monitor** looks like a TV, and works on the same principle. There are differences:

- Whereas a TV needs an antenna to receive a broadcast, a monitor doesn't, since it plugs into the processor. No signal is broadcast by the processor.
- A TV must have an amplifier and loudspeaker to relay sound. A monitor doesn't, since a processor does not emit any sound.

These are the two differences you notice immediately, but there are a few more.

Characteristics of VDUs

There are three types of standalone VDUs available. In any case, all VDUs have certain specifications which are quoted:

- **Keyboard:** integral, or separate from screen; the number and type of keys are also quoted.
- **Character set:** the number of characters that can be generated and displayed.
- **Character formation:** usually specified as the size of the matrix in which the character if formed.
- **Screen format:** either the total number of characters, or the number of lines and the number of columns that will fit on the screen. Multiply the number of lines by the number of columns, to give the total number of characters.
- **Size:** diagonal screen measurement, in the appropriate units.

You'll hear the word **cursor** being used in connection with VDUs. The cursor:

- is an indicator to the user, appearing on the screen, to signify where the data is to be entered;
- can take several forms: for example, solid rectangle or underline;
- can be blinking (flashing on and off), or stationary.

The three types of standalone VDUs are described in terms of their "intelligence," and can be **dumb**, **smart**, or **intelligent**. One characteristic of the VDU's intelligence is what facilities it gives you to change the data you have keyed before sending it to the processor. These facilities are called **editing** functions, and they comprise:

- **Tabulation:** as in a typewriter, where the cursor moves directly to a given position on the screen.
- **Clear** or **Erase screen:** clear the screen of all that is currently being displayed.
- **Delete line:** clear a given horizontal line of data from the screen.
- **Insert line:** insert a line between two other lines.
- **Delete character:** remove a character from a line.
- **Insert character:** place a character between two others.

Dumb

Dumb VDUs are used for simple data entry, and they are inexpensive.

- Data travels from the VDU to the processor a character at a time. This is called **conversational operation.**
- Editing functions may be limited to deleting a line or character only.

Smart

Smart VDUs give you the following extras:

- the full complement of editing functions, with their own separate keys, making editing simple and fast;
- **cursor control** functions, also with their own keys, so that you can move the cursor up and down, left and right, and also to HOME (the top left-hand corner of the screen);
- several **visual attributes:** the name given to features like inverse video (reversed-out display) or half-tones (different intensities of light);
- **scrolling:** the facility to move the display up or down, on or off the screen;
- data generally travels from the VDU a line at a time. This is called **message operation.**

Intelligent

Intelligent VDUs have an inbuilt microprocessor, increasing their versatility. You can now have:

- A **printer port**, which allows you to connect a printer directly to the VDU, operating independently from the processor.
- **Line graphics:** enabling simple line drawings to be produced.
- **Special character sets**, such as Greek, or mathematical symbols.
- **Protected fields:** the facility to freeze a given area of the screen, so no editing can be done on the data in that area.
- Inbuilt memory, providing storage of data before transmission to the processor.
- **Softkeys,** or **user-definable keys:** unmarked keys that you can assign to a particular task, or a sequence of other keys. You can change the assignment at any time.
- Data is generally transmitted a screenful, or page, at a time. This is called **page operation.**

Keyboards

You will encounter the word *generate* when dealing with characters and keyboards. The reason this word is used is as follows:

- VDUs have a special ROM, which stores the patterns for all the characters that can be displayed by the VDU.
- This ROM is called a **character generator ROM**.
- Pressing a key corresponds to accessing a particular memory location in the ROM, where the pattern for the character is found.

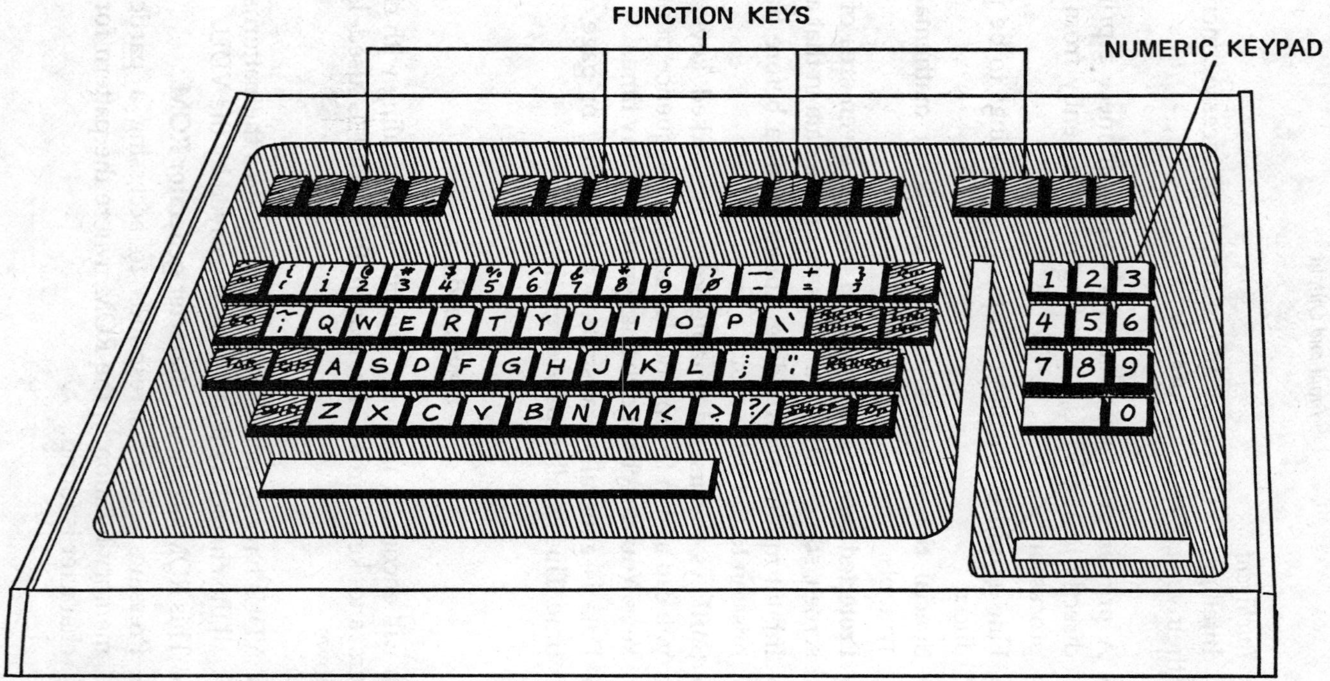
FUNCTION KEYS
NUMERIC KEYPAD

With few exceptions, VDU keyboard layouts are identical to a typewriter keyboard, as far as the location of the keys is concerned. This layout is called QWERTY, referring to the first six keys of the second row on the left-hand side.

The QWERTY layout has also been adopted in Europe, and is now the worldwide standard.

In addition to the letter keys, for data entry there are:

- a row of number keys, and above them special symbols;
- the SHIFT key, which generates capitals and special symbols;
- several keys with other symbols on them, such as . , ? + = .
- possibly a separate numeric **keyboard**, having only numbers on it, to make numeric entry easier.

Then there are the **function** keys. These enable the editing and cursor control features of the VDU. They also determine how data is transmitted to the processor, and received from it.

- Often, rather than have many separate keys, one for each function, only one key is used.
- This key is called the **CONTROL (CTRL)** key, and it is always used in conjunction with a second key.
- The normal action of the second key is modified by the action of pressing CTRL.
- CTRL is used as a shorthand way of issuing instructions.

One key that you will probably use a lot is the **CARRIAGE RETURN** key, also called **RETURN**, or **CR**.

- Since data typed at the keyboard can be of any length, the processor must be informed when the end of the data entry is reached.

- The RETURN key is recognized by the processor as a terminator.
- It is called CARRIAGE RETURN since it makes the cursor jump to the left hand edge of the screen.

Finally, depending on the VDU type, there are the softkeys, often labelled F0, F1, F2, and so on.

The way a VDU is connected to the processor depends on the VDU:

- If it is a standalone VDU, you need an appropriate interface, usually a serial one.
- If it is a separate monitor, it connects directly into the processor via a video cable.
- If it is built into the processor, no connection is required.

PRINTERS AND STATIONERY

A printer prints information received from another device, usually a computer, on to paper. It provides you with a **hard copy** (a printed record) of the information.

Printers are widely used with most computer installations, since you usually need records on paper.

All printers have certain characteristics which you should be familiar with. They are quoted in the manuals or brochures accompanying the equipment. These characteristics are:

- **Type:** impact or nonimpact.
- **Speed:** number of printed characters per second **(CPS)**.
- **Forms (paper) handling:** tractor, or pressure or friction feed; single sheet, continuous, or paper roll stationery.
- **Forms (paper) size:** size of the paper (length × width).

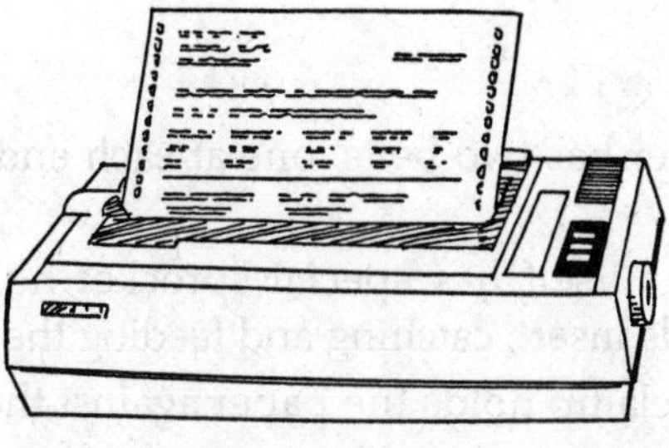

- **Printing density/Character spacing:** number of characters printed per horizontal inch **(CPI)**. Can also be specified as the number of characters per line **(CPL)**.
- **Line spacing:** number of printed lines per vertical inch **(LPI)**.
- **Character set:** number of characters that can be printed.

Other characteristics may be quoted, such as:

- **Throughput:** printed line per minute **(LPM)**.
- **Paper slew rate:** rate of paper feed in inches per second **(IPS)**.
- **Tab speed:** time taken to tab a given number of spaces **(CPS)**.
- **Multiple-copy:** the number of sheets of paper that can be printed on at the same time.

Impact printers are very much like typewriters:

- They rely on a mechanical force to transfer the character onto paper.
- They are used in conjunction with a ribbon.

Non-impact printers rely on other means:

- Heat, electricity, or jets of ink produce the characters.

Tractor feed:

- The printer has two belts, one at each end, with protruding studs.
- The paper itself has special sprocket holes, into which these studs insert, catching and feeding the paper through.
- A spring clamp holds the paper against the belt.
- A motor turns the belts, thereby feeding the paper past the printing head.

Pressure or friction feed:

- much like the ones found on a typewriter, where roller wheels are used to feed the paper.

Impact Printers

The two most common types of impact printers are **dot-matrix** and **daisywheel**. Both of these are character printers, since they only print one character at a time.

Dot-matrix printers are so called because they build a character, be it a letter, number, or symbol, as a matrix or array of dots, using very fine needles that impact on the ribbon.

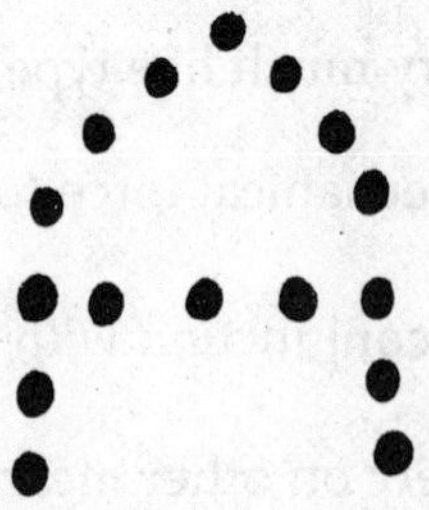

Two additional specifications of dot-matrix printers are:

- **Matrix size:** the size of the printing head matrix, expressed as the number of rows by the number of columns; typical sizes are 5×7, 7×7, 9×7.
- **Printhead life:** the number of characters that the printhead will print in its life, typically expressed in multiples of 100 million printed characters.

Dot-matrix printers have speeds ranging from 30 to 600 CPS.

Most dot-matrix printers are controlled by their own microprocessor, which relieves the central processor of some tasks. It gives them an inbuilt intelligence, which provides you with many more features:

- **Bidirectional printing** (printing while the printing head moves to the right and on the return trip).
- **Graphics** (high-resolution drawings composed of dots). Created by variable column/line spacing, and activation of the individual needles in the printhead.

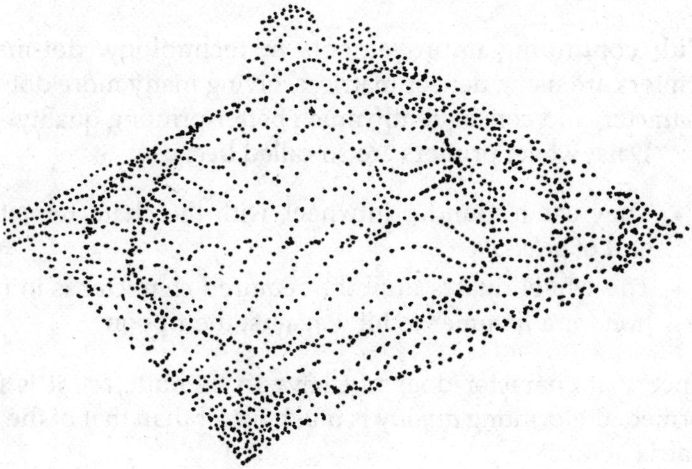

- Selectable printing density and line spacing.
- Forms control (variable page lengths, vertical and horizontal tabulation).
- Interchangeable special character ROMs allowing foreign language accents and characters, special characters and symbols, such as mathematical ones.
- Self-diagnosis routines (the printer can check itself and report any errors, such as no paper).
- Upper- and lower-case letters, emboldening, underlining.
- True **descenders** (the part of the character that appears below the baseline).

Some printers also offer:

- **Proportional** spacing (where each character takes up only the space it needs; for example, the letter *i* needs less space than the letter *m*).

as opposed to:

- **Monospacing** (fixed amount of space taken up irrespective of the character).

With continuing improvements in technology, dot-matrix printers are using denser matrices, giving many more dots per character, and consequently much better printing quality.

Daisywheel printers are so called because:

- They use a round printwheel, with the characters at the end of *petals*.
- The wheel rotates until the required character is in position for a hammer to hit it against the ribbon.

Since that character does not have to be built, *i.e.*, it is fully formed, the printing quality is much better than that of the dot-matrix.

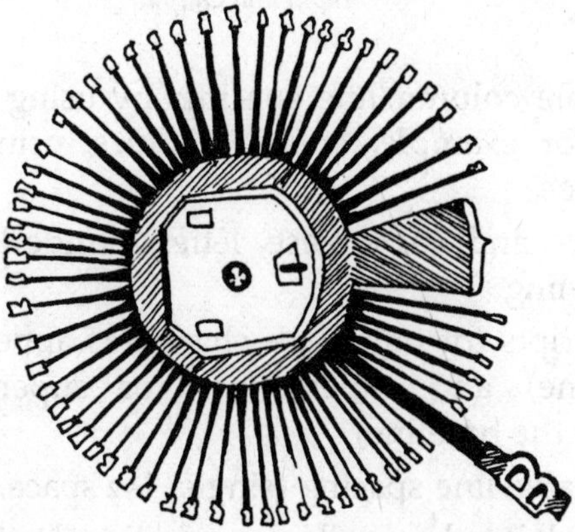

Daisywheels are made of plastic or metal, and are available in pica, elite, or proportional spacing.

- **Pica:** 10 pitch, or 10 characters printed per horizontal inch.
- **Elite:** 12 pitch, or 12 characters per inch.
- 15 characters per inch is also available.

Paper is fed in singly in sheets, or automatically by a multi-sheet form feeder, or by tractors.

One other additional characteristic is quoted:

- Printwheel type:
  plastic—usually with 96 characters.
  metal—88, 92, or 96 characters.

Typical features include:

- Speeds: 15–55 CPS.
- Varieties of fonts available, together with special symbols, different languages, by simply selecting the required wheel.
- Daisywheel printers take A4 sheets.
- Bidirectional printing.
- Two-color printing, using two-color ribbons.

- Variable column/line spacing: by using this facility you can, for example, create graphics, using dots to print pictures.
- Upper- and lower-case letters, underlining, and emboldening.
- Subscripts (or inferiors—characters appearing below the baseline) and superscripts (or superiors—appearing above the baseline).
- Selectable line spacing (single, 1½ space, etc.).
- Metal daisywheels allow proportional printing.

Daisywheel printers can use both single sheet and continuous stationery.

Printers can be further classified as:

- **RO** (**R**eceive **O**nly).
- **KSR** (**K**eyboard **S**end **R**eceive): the latter type has an inbuilt keyboard, allowing it to be used as a terminal, or as a typewriter when not connected to the processor.

Most printers are of the RO type.

All printers accept the standard serial or parallel interfaces, and some also accept non-standard ones, to be used with specific makes of computer.

Ribbons are either contained in spools, or in cartridges, and may be fiber or carbon.

- **Carbon:** thin plastic film coated with carbon offering very good quality print, but rather a short life.
- **Fiber:** textile treated with ink; not as neat as the carbon, but cheaper and long-lasting.

Another type of impact printer is the **line printer**, so called because it prints a line at a time. It is expensive and only suitable for high printing volumes; it is also very fast, with a throughput of between 300 and 3000 LPM.

Nonimpact Printers

Two common types of nonimpact printers are **thermal** and **electrosensitive** printers.

Thermal printers are compact, inexpensive, and quiet in operation.

- They use heat to create a character on special heat-sensitive paper.
- A special printing head is used, composed of tiny electric heaters, arranged in a dot-matrix pattern.
- Speeds: 10–80 CPS.
- Forms handling: roll, treated paper.
- Matrix size: 5 × 7 (typical).
- Character set: foreign language, special symbols, graphics.
- Printing density: 16–132 CPL.

Thermal printers are not suitable for large volumes of printing. Another drawback: The paper may be expensive and difficult to get.

Electrosensitive printers offer much the same advantages as thermal printers, although they may be more noisy; again, the paper may be expensive and hard to get.

- They use a special metal foil-backed paper. The printhead has wires, called electrodes, which are used to create a spark between them and the paper. The spark burns the paper, leaving a tiny spot. The character consists of a dot-matrix of these spots.
- Speeds: up to 160 CPS.
- Forms handling: roll, treated paper.

- Matrix size: 5 × 8 (typical).
- Printing density: 20–80 CPL.

There are other types of nonimpact printers, but these are large and expensive, and are suitable only for high printing volumes.

- **Ink jet:** these use tiny electrically charged particles of ink, which are squirted onto paper using electric fields.
- **Page printers:** these use electrostatic (like photocopiers) or laser techniques to print a page at a time, achieving a throughput of up to 20000 LPM.

Stationery

The most usual stationery for printers is paper, and it may be:

- **Single sheet:** such as the standard A4, which can be preprinted with your company or other details.
- **Continuous:** where the sheets are held together by perforations (this also may be known as fanfold) plain or preprinted.
- **Single or multi-part:** the latter having carbon interleaving for multiple copies. The carbon is called **OTC**—one time carbon—as it is used only once.
- **Plain or ruled:** the latter having alternative lines in a different shade.
- **With or without side perforations:** the former having a ½″ strip on either side with sprocket holes for tractor feed.

There are many sizes of paper available. Consult your computer stationery catalogue for the various sizes. When quoting sizes, it is **drop** (height) first, then width.

You can also get a large variety of self-adhesive labels for jobs like mail shots, printing product labels, etc.

DISKS

A disk is a device that stores large amounts of data in a way that allows fast access to it. The amount of data stored on a disk is also expressed in K or M (Kilobytes or **Megabytes**).

Disks are useful because:

- The processor's RAM (Random Access Memory) is not suitable for permanent storage, since its contents are lost when power is turned off. A disk does not lose its contents when power is turned off.
- Much more can be stored on a disk than can be stored in RAM.

The term *disk* or *diskette* refers to the media and the hardware that makes it work is called a **disk drive.**

Disks are classifed as:

- **Floppy** or **hard.**
- **Fixed** or **exchangeable.**
- Floppies are so called because they consist of a flexible plastic disk contained in a square plastic envelope. Floppy disks are always exchangeable.
- Hard disks, as the name implies, are made of aluminium or ceramic material. Hard disks may be fixed or exchangeable.
- Fixed disks may not be removed from their controlling hardware and housing; therefore, one disk stores all the data.

- Exchangeable disks may be removed, so you can use different disks to store different data. They may be used as required, and stored away when finished.

Data is stored on the disks in the same way as music on audio cassettes. The surface of the disk is coated with magnetic compound, and electric signals representing the data are fed on to the surface using a read/write head.

The disk is notionally divided into concentric rings, called **tracks.**

- The track is like a track on an LP.
- Tracks have a number associated with them; this number is called the **address.**

Each track is in turn divided into equal-sized **sectors**. The sector determines the smallest amount of data that can be accessed by the processor. This division may be done in two ways:

- **hard sectoring:** the sectors are identified by physical markers, such as holes in the hub of the disk;
- **soft sectoring:** the sectors are identified by a prerecorded code at the start of each sector.

Since each sector has a number, together with the track address, it is possible to access any block of data by referring to its address.

In this sense, disks are like LPs—if you want to select a particular tune, you move the arm to the right track. When considering disks, there are certain specifications with which you should be familiar:

- **size** (diameter of the disk in inches or millimeters [mm]);
- **unformatted capacity** (K or M): the total disk capacity;

- **formatted capacity** (K or M): the space available for data storage, which will always be less than the unformatted capacity;
- **sectoring:** hard or soft.

Other specifications which may be quoted are more technical in nature. You may still be interested though:

- **rotation speed (RPM);**
- **latency time** (milliseconds): related to the rotation speed, in that it is the time taken for one disk revolution (a millisecond is 1/1000 of a second, and is abbreviated to **ms**);
- **average latency:** one-half of the latency;
- **seek time** (ms): the time taken to position the read/write head to a given track;
- **access time** (ms): seek time plus latency;
- **data transfer rate** (Kilobytes per second): speed at which the data is read or written.

Floppy Disks

Floppies come in two standard sizes: 5¼″ (133mm) and 8″ (203mm). The 5¼″ is sometimes called a *minifloppy*.

Floppies can also be:

- **single-sided** (SS) (only one side used for encoding);
- **double-sided** (DS) (both sides used);
- **single-density;**
- **double-density** (roughly double the capacity of a single-density).

You can get four varieties of floppies:

- single-sided, single-density;
- single-sided, double-density;

- double-sided, single-density;
- double-sided, double-density.

The type you get will depend on the controlling hardware and the disk operating system (DOS).

Here are some typical figures for floppies:

	5¼"	8"
• capacity (SS)	200K	500K
capacity (DS)	400K	1M

- new disks have been developed that hold 1M on 5¼", and 3.13M on an 8";
- rotation speed: 300—360 RPM;
- sectoring: hard or soft;
- sector size: 256 or 512 bytes;
- seek times: 3–50 ms;
- data transfer rate: 150 Kilobytes per second.

There are two cutouts in the envelope, one circular, in the middle (A), the other one oblong, to the side (B). The disk is rotated by two clamps that grip it through the circular hub.

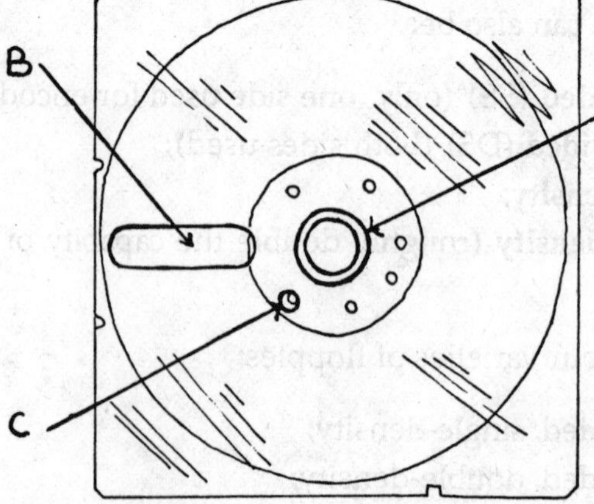

The read/write head moves along the oblong slot to access the data. There will also be a third, smaller hole (C); this is used to signify the start of the sectors.

Advantages

- Disks are cheap, and the drives inexpensive.
- Easy to store, because of their small size.
- Removable—as many disks as needed can be used for storage.
- Double-sided, double-density disks provide large storage facilities.

Disadvantages

- Since the head is direct contact, there are problems with wear—floppies do not last very long.
- To avoid serious wear problems, the disks are comparatively slow.
- Prone to damage by user.
- Double-sided, double-density disks are expensive, due to closer manufacturing tolerances.

Hard Disks

Hard disks are used in applications that require large data storage facilities, and very fast access to the data.

A popular type of fixed hard disk technology is the **Winchester**, developed by IBM but refined by other manufacturers.

This is the way Winchesters work:

- The disk is in a hermetically sealed housing, so no dust can get in.
- Inside is an air-recirculation unit, which maintains a constant air pressure inside the housing, and also filters any dust from getting in.

- The disk rotates at high speed.
- The read/write head floats a tiny distance above the disk, supported by a cushion of air.

Although exchangeable Winchesters are being developed, they are for the most part fixed, and come in 5¼″, 8″, and 14″ diameters.

ADVANTAGES
- Fast.
- Compact—large amounts of data stored in small size.
- Since there is no contact, no wear problems, hence a longer life and greater reliability.

DISADVANTAGE
- It is difficult to make backups, because the disk can't be removed, and because of the amount of data stored (a 10M disk is equivalent to about 50 floppies).

Here are some typical figures for Winchesters:

• Size:	5¼″	8″	14″
• Capacity:	6M	20M	40M

- Sectoring: soft.
- Rotation speed: 1500–3600 RPM.
- Data transfer rate: 1000 Kilobytes per second.

OTHER USEFUL DEVICES

MODEMS

Sometimes it is necessary for one or more processors, or processors and peripherals, to communicate with each other over long distances. Some typical situations:

- a small computer is used as an intelligent terminal to a remote computer, to access daily share prices or train timetables;
- a terminal is used as an intelligent telephone, automatically dialing numbers, redialing if no response, using phone numbers stored on disk.

One way to achieve this is to use the telephone lines; to do this:

- the data from the processor must be converted to a form suitable for transmission by telephone lines;
- the received data must be converted to be compatible with the peripheral.

This conversion in both cases is done by a **MODEM**, which is an acronym for **MOdulator/DEModulator**. A MODEM converts computer-type signals to the most efficient form for transmitting over phone lines. Modems come in two types:

- **Acoustically coupled:** the processor or peripheral has sucker-type outlets where a telephone headset can be placed. All that is necessary is to dial a number, which establishes a connection, and place the telephone headset on the suckers.
- **Hardwired:** the modem is part of the electronics—there is no external connection to be made, except connecting it directly into a phone line.

In both cases, the modem must be connected to the processor via a suitable interface. If you get a modem, it must be approved by the body governing telephone transmissions, and it must be compatible with your processor or interface.

MODEMS can transmit synchronously or asynchronously:

- synchronous transmission generally gives you low transmission speeds;
- asynchronous transmission gives you high transmission speeds.

Acoustically-coupled MODEMS can only be used at the low end of transmission speeds, because of losses in the coupling.

Computer Graphics

Plotters

A plotter is an output device—use it if data is to be displayed in the form of graphics or diagrams. Since the display is on paper, you get a hard copy.

The advantages of using plotters instead of ordinary printers that can do graphics are:

- they are more accurate, faster, quieter, and more versatile for certain kinds of graphics applications, than printers; examples are scientific/engineering drawings;
- they can accommodate large sizes of paper, different colors of pens, and draw on different types of media.

The most common type of plotter is the **flatbed**:

- the paper is electrostatically held flat on a table;
- one or more pens move along the paper to produce the drawing.

The pen is moved by two motors:

- in the horizontal, or X direction;
- in the vertical, or Y direction.

By specifying how much the pen is to be moved in either direction, a drawing is produced.

The drawing pen or pens may be:

- filled with ink, felt-tipped, and come in several colors.

The drawing pen or pens can also be:

- raised from or lowered to the paper, either manually or by software control.

Drawings may be produced on:

- paper, acetate, or film;
- different sizes of material.

Some plotter specifications are:

- **plotting area:** length of X and Y directions or size of paper accommodated (A2);
- **plotting speed** (cm or mm/sec): the speed at which the pen moves (50 cm/sec);
- **resolution** (mm): the smallest change possible in a given direction (the ability to distinguish two separate points) (0.1 mm).

Note the following:

- character fonts may be available, in different languages, or with special symbols;
- plotters are digital machines, and the only moving parts are the **stepper-motors**, which are microprocessor-controlled.

Stepper-motors are different from ordinary electric motors; they do not rotate continuously, but in small steps, one step at a time.

Graphic Tablets

A **graphic tablet** is an input device—you use it if you want to create a drawing without having to calculate data points or coordinates. In effect, it is an electronic sketchpad.

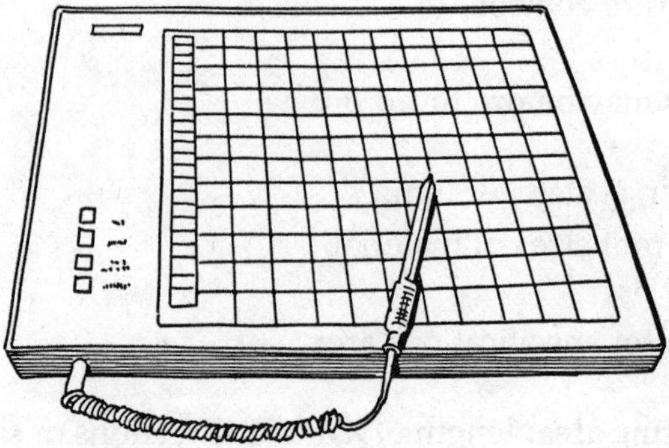

A graphic tablet works in much the same way as a plotter:

- a picture is specified in terms of points in the X and Y directions;
- a pen, called a stylus, moves along the tablet;
- the tablet senses the position of the stylus, and converts this position into coordinates.

A graphic tablet allows you to:

- create a graphic display by tracing over a picture;
- enter a picture directly into the processor, without measurements or pressing keys at a keyboard.

In addition, some tablets have special software, which lets you:

- use pre-stored symbols without drawing them;
- select the size of the display window;
- store and edit the display.

The most important specification for a graphic tablet is its resolution.

With both plotters and graphic tablets, the interfaces are generally the standard ones, either RS 232 or IEEE 488. Some manufacturers supply their own interfaces, to preserve compatibility with their other product lines.

One very useful variation on the graphics tablet is a **data-entry pad**. This device can simplify the entry of data to such an extent that it can make a standard keyboard unnecessary in certain situations.

This is how it works:

- The tablet is subdivided into as many smaller areas (squares, rectangles) as needed, and the perimeter coordinates stored.
- Under software control, every box on the tablet corresponds to a separate item of data—a name, an often-used description, or anything else you decide to allocate.
- To select this data item, you simply place the stylus inside the box. The software senses its location, and then generates the required data, which is then used by the processor.
- The number of boxes and their contents can be changed as often as needed; a lot of formats can be stored for later use.

Graphic Displays

Graphic data can also be displayed on VDUs, and there are two means used to generate a picture: raster scanning and vector scanning.

Raster Scanning

Ordinary TVs work by **raster scanning:**

- The term refers to the action of the CRT's electron beam, which sweeps horizontally across the visual area at a rate of 50 or 60 times a second.
- The paths along which the beams sweep are called **scan lines.**

Each scan line is divided into tiny picture cells—**pixels**—any one of which can be located by the processor:

- Under a program's control, each pixel is switched on or off, to black, white, or a shade of gray, or to a color.
- An image is created by selecting the appropriate pixels, and turning them on to the required color.
- To change the image, a new set of pixels must be created.
- Images can be animated by turning the pixels off, selecting new ones which have been moved, and switching them on again.
- Raster scan graphics can be generated on ordinary VDUs, providing the appropriate software is included, and that facility was allowed for in the design.

The resolution (ability to distinguish two separate pixels) is limited by the number of pixels on the screen, and the number of scan lines.

ADVANTAGE

- Relative cheapness and ease of use.

DISADVANTAGES

- It is not always suitable for drawing diagonals—they appear with jagged edges.
- It is not always suitable for professional animation, because of the slow scan rate.

Vector Scanning

Vector scanning offers much more scope for graphics applications where precision and speed are essential. There is no horizontal scanning, and no pixels; the drawing is created by moving the electron beam in any direction, just as you would move a pen in any direction. The actual positions are specified by coordinates, as in a plotter.

ADVANTAGES

- Much higher resolution gives much better image.
- Color and monochrome displays are generated as easily as with raster methods.
- A lot of specialist and general software is available.

DISADVANTAGE

- Special graphics VDUs are needed for vector graphics, and hence the prices are high.

Vector scanning is extensively used in **CAD (Computer-Aided Design)** and **CAM (Computer-Aided Manufacture)** applications, because of the ease of creating and manipulating three-dimensional images.

Whatever your graphics application, remember that the more specialized the application, the more likely it will be that you will need more facilities on your VDU, and more specialized software.

Magnetic Tape

Magnetic tape (magtape) is a convenient storage medium, used when:

- large amounts of data have to be stored inexpensively;
- rapid access to the data is not important.

Magnetic tape is a **sequential access** medium, which is the opposite of what a disk is (**direct access**).

Sequential access:

- to access any item of data in a sequential medium, all the preceding items must be accessed;
- you can best see how a sequential medium works by considering a music cassette: to get to a given tune, all the preceding tunes must be skipped over.

An advantage of using this type of medium:

- it is very cheap, and the hardware is cheaper than disk drives, so you can store a lot of data at a low cost.

The main disadvantage of magtape:

- the slow access speed.

The most common application of magtape:

- creating archives—copies of data that are stored, to be used if the originals are lost.

Measurement and Control

You've seen that computers can be used to measure physical entities, and can act as controlling devices. This is accomplished as follows:

- The processor can only operate on electrical signals, hence all physical entities must ultimately be reduced to this form.

- Physical entities, such as pressure or temperature, must be first converted into their electrical equivalent. This electrical equivalent is called an **analog** signal.
- Devices that convert physical entities to analog signals are called **transducers**. A microphone is a transducer—it converts sound waves into electrical signals.

Processors can only operate on binary signals:

- The analog signal must be converted to a digital signal.
- This conversion is done by a device called an **Analog-to-Digital Converter (A/D or ADC)**.
- The ADC is an integrated circuit, whose output can be linked directly to the processor.

Remember that two separate conversions must take place for the processor to measure physical entities:

- The entity being measured is converted into an electrical equivalent (analog), using a transducer.
- The analog signal is converted into a digital signal, using an A/D.

This process is reversible:

- A processor can issue a digital signal, consisting of one or more bits, which is then converted to an analog signal using a **Digital-to-Analog (DAC or D/A) Converter**.
- Another transducer converts the signal to a physical entity. (For example, a loudspeaker converts electrical signals to sound waves.)

How is a computer used for control? Consider a simple case of a computer-controlled thermostat, which keeps the temperature at a predefined setting:

- The processor inputs data from a thermometer, using an A/D.
- The software compares the input value to the preset value, and a decision is made based on this comparison.
- One decision might be to open a valve—the processor sends a byte, which is then converted by a DAC into a signal that the valve motor can operate on.
- The processor reads the temperature again, and the whole process is repeated, until the right temperature is reached.
- The processor performs these actions many thousands of times each second. If the application demands it, minute changes can be intercepted and acted on, much faster and more accurately than by people.

5
TYPES OF SOFTWARE AND HARDWARE

There are two types of software: **applications software,** and **systems software.**

APPLICATIONS SOFTWARE

Applications software is software that does something for you. The user of applications software is the person who will get some benefit out of the computer.

Anybody who uses the computer is called a user. Applications software is developed to be **user-friendly**—to make it as easy as possible to use the software and the computer as a whole.

User-Friendliness

The characteristics of user-friendly software are:

- Thorough **error-checking:** this means that the program will check and validate any data that you give it; for example, if a number is needed, only numbers will be accepted (no letters or other symbols). You are always given a chance to do something again, should you make a mistake.

- **Display layout:** all the information that you need is displayed on the screen in a pleasing way.
- **Dialogs:** if you have to provide data to the program, you are **prompted**, by messages or interrogations; if you do something incorrectly, you are told so by a message—in effect, you have a conversation with the program.
- **Menus:** in a program that does many tasks, these provide you with a convenient way of choosing what has to be done. So that you don't have to learn a lot of **commands**, you are presented with the choices in a list—you call up a task by keying in a letter or number, just like in a restaurant.

SYSTEMS SOFTWARE

Systems software is software that does something with the computer, not for the user. Its main purpose is to allow applications software to be used on the computer.

Operating System

The most important part of software in this category is the operating system. It:

- is supplied by the manufacturer of the processor;
- is a set of programs written in the processor's natural language;
- is a go-between between you, the processor, and the applications software.

The operating system is responsible for one thing: making the computer as easy as possible to use:

- it informs you of any errors that occur with the processor, peripherals, or programs;
- it provides you with a repertoire of simple commands, for functions which would otherwise be complicated.

Operating systems are usually installed in ROMs, when the processor is built. When ROMs hold other software, such as a language, this software is collectively called **firmware.**

Disk Operating Systems

One important subset of the operating system is the disk operating system, commonly called **DOS**. Any processor that uses disks will have a DOS. The DOS is responsible for:

- reading and writing to the disk.

When reading data from, and writing data to disks, the DOS must:

- move the read/write head to the appropriate track/sector;
- check and report on any errors that may occur during access.

The DOS is also responsible for file management. Consider data organized in the following way:

- A single piece of data is called an **element**. For example, the number *6*.
- A group of related elements is called a **field**. For example, the numbers *65108* can be a field, as can the word *APPLE*.

- A group of related fields is called a **record.**
- A group of related records is called a **file.**

Files are notional entities, conceptually the same as any other file. On a correspondence file, for example, the records are letters. All a file does is impose a structure on data.

File management consists of:

- creating files on the disk by allocating space;
- giving files names;
- erasing or deleting files from the disk;
- keeping a **directory**, or catalog, of the disk's contents. A directory is like a book index: to see where a file is on the disk, DOS looks at this index.

Many methods have been developed to construct files, to organize their contents, and to read and write data to them.

The widespread use and versatility of disks as a storage medium is due to DOS allowing direct access to data.

Direct access means that any record may be accessed individually. The user doesn't first have to access any preceding records. Because of the nature of the disk, data can be accessed directly.

Remember, disks are like music recordings:

- as with phono records, to select a particular item, you just move the arm;
- with a music tape, you can record, and play back, and also over-record, anything already on it;
- a disk is coated with the same material that a tape is made of, thereby giving you exactly the same facilities.

A disk can store either data files or programs, or both.

One other function of the DOS is the **initialization,** or **formatting** of disks.

When DOS initializes a disk, it:

- imposes an organizational structure onto the disk and maps out the areas where data can be stored;
- establishes where the directory is located, and writes any other data that may be needed. For example, DOS itself may be stored on the disk.

Utilities

- Utility programs are supplied with the processor by the manufacturer, as part of the system's software.
- These programs are used only when needed—they are not an integral part of the operating system.

Two utilities you'll come across are the **copy** and **sort programs.**

Copy Program

This program enables you to make copies of disks—in much the same way as you would copy music cassettes:

- A sector or track is read from the original disk, and written to the duplicate disk. This procedure is repeated until the entire contents of the original disk have been transferred to the duplicate disk.
- The copy program is used to make security, or backup, copies of disks; should you lose or damage a disk, you will always have a duplicate.
- Almost every computer manufacturer supplies the copy utility as part of the system.

Sort Program

It is sometimes necessary to order or arrange the contents of a file into a predetermined order or sequence. For example, arranging names into alphabetical order.

- The sort program does this ordering according to one or more **keys**. Beware—these keys are different from the ones on a keyboard. A sort key is a field within a record of a file, by which that file is ordered. For example, if sorting a file of names into alphabetical order, the surname is the sort key.
- Whether a sort utility is supplied depends on the manufacturer; in any case, these programs are widely available.

One very popular operating system for small computers is **CP/M** (**C**ontrol **P**rogram/**M**icroprocessors). It is available on most small machines, and this means that programs written on one computer can be used on another, providing both have CP/M. Although this has not proved to be totally successful, CP/M is the first attempt to standardize, and hence make easier, the use of computer software.

TYPES OF COMPUTERS

Computers are traditionally classified into three categories: **microcomputers**, **minicomputers**, and **mainframes**. Here is a guide to their major features:

Microcomputers

- are small, desktop machines, used by one person at a time—inexpensive, and easy to use;
- use floppy disks, or small Winchesters, standard microprocessors, and have a memory capacity of around 100K.

Minicomputers

- are larger than micros, but not bigger than a filing cabinet, and not much more difficult to use;

- use large Winchesters, or other hard disks, and have a memory capacity of several hundred K;
- allow use by several people at the same time, because of their memory size and more sophisticated software.

Mainframes

- are very large machines, occupying a room to themselves, which require special personnel to run them;
- have a memory capacity of several megabytes, and use disks with several thousand megabytes capacity;
- are extremely fast, and are used for the most demanding processing and storage requirements. They are also very expensive.

The difference between the three types is measured in terms of their size, price, and power. Power is defined by:

- **architecture:** how the processor is designed;
- **speed:** how fast the program works;
- **memory:** how much is available for the processor;
- **peripherals:** how many can be accommodated, their speed and size;
- **data storage:** how much disk storage is available, and how fast data can be accessed.

When the first minis appeared in the mid-sixties, the manufacturers called them *mini,* since they were smaller than mainframes. When micros appeared in the mid-seventies, they were so called because of their relative size. The frame of reference is not appropriate, but by tradition the names have remained. You may have problems categorizing a machine, since the dividing lines are not well defined.

Recently, a new type of computer has appeared—the **home**, or **personal** computer. This computer:

- is very inexpensive and easy to use;
- has a memory capacity typically between 5K and 64K;
- uses a domestic TV as a VDU, and an ordinary cassette player as a storage device;
- usually has very good graphics, color, and music facilities.

HELPFUL LANGUAGE

When using either applications or systems software, and any type of hardware, you'll come across a variety of terms; here are a few:

- If programs are stored on disk, they are **loaded** (transferred from disk to memory) before use. The DOS takes care of this. To use a program, you must have it in memory.
- After it is loaded, it is **run**, or **executed**. This means that the instructions that make up the program are read one after the other, and carried out.
- If there is an error in the program, it is a **bug**, and the task of removing bugs is **debugging**.
- To make the computer even easier to use, there are certain programs that are run before any applications. With no help from you, the computer "picks itself up by its bootstraps"—this is called **booting**. Booting is simply the computer bringing itself into a certain state by means of its own actions.
- If a bug causes the computer to stop working, you have a **crash** on your hands.
- You can have **fatal errors,** or **nonfatal errors**. Fatal errors mean you can't proceed with anything.
- With nonfatal errors, you can sometimes restart your work. You can have **warm starts** where possibly no data

has been lost, or **cold starts**, where you have to start all over again, usually by switching off first.

- **Defaults:** this term applies to data values. The **default value** is what the program takes on in the absence of any entries from you. You can, however, override defaults any time, by entering data yourself.
- When a peripheral is **on-line**, it is connected to the processor, and it is also receiving data from it, or transmitting data to it.
- A peripheral is **off-line** if it is not connected to the processor, and is not communicating with it. Some peripherals can still be used when they're off-line—for example, a KSR printer can also be used as a typewriter.

6
ANALYZING THE NEEDS

There is only one reason for getting a computer:

- as an aid to professional expertise.

Here is a guide to your approach to computers:

- Read as much as possible. There are many publications, books, and periodicals.
- Become familiar with the jargon and some of the concepts.
- Talk to other people in your position, or other people who already have a computer.
- Avoid consultants unless in dire need. They are very expensive, and are suitable only for large-scale projects.
- Get advice and help from professional or business counseling services, if any, in your field.
- Don't talk to suppliers or salesmen yet. They will be a hindrance.
- Try to do as much as you can yourself, and don't rush in.

Justifying a Computer

Two conditions must be met to justify computerization:

1. some sort of benefit must be realized, be it financial, procedural, or some other unquantifiable one;
2. a computer is the only way to realize this benefit.

Consider the first condition:

- determine what problems are to be solved, and which ones are to be solved first.

If you do this, you will find out a lot about what you do, and how you do it. This sounds trivial, but it is vital that you know what procedures apply in your work.

- Get as many numbers as you can. Quantify what can be quantified, since this will make things easier later. Don't rely solely on averages—you will need maximums and minimums as well.
- If possible, cost the methods and procedures you use.
- Write everything down.

You will have a good summary of your operations. Now determine what benefits you want to see, and consider the second condition in this light.

- Don't rely on prices of computers as a guide. Raw processing power is cheap, and you get a lot for it.
- By the same token, don't be misled by all this power. Can it do something for you?
- Remember that, in most cases, the speed at which processing is done depends on the speed at which data is entered and results produced.

Carefully consider the costs of computerizing. You'll find that:

- in some cases software is more expensive than hardware;
- there are one-off and on-going costs;
- one-off costs: hardware and software purchase, installation;
- on-going: consumables, such as diskettes and paper.

Also remember that a sloppy way of doing things manually, transferred to a computer, will result in a sloppy way of doing things on a computer.

Finally:

- Don't wait for technology to improve, or prices to drop, unless you have strong grounds. You have to start somewhere.
- By making the right choice in the first place, you should have a system that will do what you want it to for a long time.

7
RECOGNIZING THE SOLUTIONS

INTRODUCTION

If you think a computer can help you, remember that software:

- is very much more important than hardware.
- will become increasingly important as time goes on;
- defines the uses and usefulness of a computer;
- determines the ease of use and flexibility of the hardware facilities offered.

When considering software, remember that once you find what you need, the hardware to support it will follow naturally, since to a large extent software is still machine-dependent—or at least dependent on the available standard operating systems.

However, don't neglect the hardware:

- examine other available software for your processor;
- some computers have a large range of software, others haven't—this should influence your decision;
- you are likely to need more software as time goes by.

CHOICES

When buying software, you can choose from **packages** or **tailor-made custom systems**. Software may be written by:

- **software houses:** companies that write both packages and custom systems, employing **programmers** and **systems analysts;**
- **systems houses:** companies that advise on and sell hardware, coordinated with software, in the same way as software houses;
- **contract programmers:** people who take on a project on a contract basis, coordinated by specialist agencies.

Packages

A package is a ready-to-use, prewritten **suite** of programs complete with documentation.

Packages:

- concentrate on applications where the requirements are well defined, by legislation or generally accepted methods or principles;
- are easy to get for science and related fields, where requirements are more clearly defined;
- are more difficult in commerce, where requirements may be less clear—sometimes the specification tells you what can't be done, rather than what can be done;
- must appeal to the largest cross section of users, so they are general, and compromises will have been made;
- are intended for bulk sale, so prices are lower than equivalent custom systems;
- won't necessarily perform a given job in exactly the way you do, so be prepared for possible tailoring;

- represent the best value for money when you buy general-purpose ones;
- vary in price; beware of ones that seem too cheap or too expensive for what they do.

Tailor-Made

Tailor-made, or **custom** systems, as the name implies, are written as one-off jobs to suit individual needs.

Since the system will generally be sold only once, all the overheads will have to be absorbed in the price—hence the high cost.

Also, all the resources that the software house has available will be used, so it may take some time to write.

What should you look for when investigating custom systems?

- make sure there are no suitable packages available;
- if you find a package that is reasonably close to what you need, see how much it will be to tailor it;
- check with trade or professional people in your field; they may know of packages or sources of information;
- don't be shocked when you learn the price.

FINANCING

One other area that may cause problems is the financing of computer systems. There are several ways of buying systems, and which one you choose will depend on many factors. Here are some points to bear in mind:

- make use of whatever allowances against corporation tax are available;

- predict your future needs, and assess how long you might keep your system, and how you might want to upgrade;
- get advice from various finance houses, which are generally attached to clearing or merchant banks—it pays to compare rates and terms and select the best;
- remember that computers depreciate quickly, and a lot.

There are five ways you can get a system: outright purchase, leasing, hire-purchase, bank loan or rental.

Outright Purchase

- Easiest.
- You might find something better to do with the money, unless there is an immediate financial benefit.
- The system is yours, with minimum documentation, and is an asset.
- You might have problems in disposing of it when the time comes.

Leasing

- The equipment may be disposed of after the period of the lease.
- The equipment is neither an asset nor a liability, and doesn't appear on the Balance Sheet.
- It may prove expensive if the system is small and the interest rates high.
- You can claim the full monthly payments against taxes.
- Make sure you deal with a company that has experience in computers, as they will be more helpful.

Hire-Purchase

- Also called lease purchase, it offers the same facilities as leasing.
- The equipment becomes yours at the end of the period.
- Interest rates are sometimes a little higher than those for leasing.
- A down-payment or deposit is usually required; often about 10% of the price.

Bank Loan

- Check if there are any special schemes available from the bank. If so, interest rates could be lower, and loans could be comparatively easy to get.

Rental

- Shop around, to get the best deal; the system may never be yours, but you can experiment with it before deciding.
- More interest will be taken in you as a customer after the system is installed.
- Check that maintenance is included in the rental fee.

Don't forget: you'll still have to get the software. Remember:

- software is still seen as an intangible item, so to finance houses it may represent no real security;
- you'll probably have to purchase it outright;
- in some cases it is never really yours, since it was sold to you on a permanent license.

Second-User

Most people buy their machines brand new, direct from the factory. There are also second-hand machines, and this market, also called the **second-user** market, is getting bigger.

You may consider a second-user system, but remember:

- There are no moving parts in the processor, so the price doesn't depend on how much use the system has had.
- The price mostly depends on the state of new technology.
- There isn't the same enthusiasm in selling second-user machines as there is with new ones. After-sales support could be almost nonexistent.
- You have to be familiar with the machine, how to install it, and how to use it. You will get no help with this.
- Maintenance could also be a problem: investigate this area thoroughly before making a decision.

Second-user machines are advertised in various trade journals, and there are a few brokers as well. As with any second-hand purchase, the rule is: caveat emptor.

BUREAUS

A computer bureau is like the local photocopying shop; its function is to allow sharing of an expensive resource among many users.

Bureaus can be independent companies, or can be backed by larger corporations, such as banks or computer companies.

Bureaus can be used in two main ways: **batch**, or **on-line**.

- **Batch:** you prepare your data and bring it to the bureau. A day or two later, the processed results are ready for collection. Sometimes bureaus can arrange for collection and delivery.

- **On-line:** you have a VDU, and perhaps a printer, at your end. Data is entered, and results received at your location. Your terminal is connected to the bureau via a phone line.

There seems to be more against using a bureau than for it.

ADVANTAGES

- Expertise in computers is readily available.
- No capital outlay is required.
- A smooth and less complicated approach to computerization.
- Better after-sales support than from computer suppliers.
- Access to sophisticated software that may not be available on smaller machines.

DISADVANTAGES

- For the price of the bureau's services, you can buy a computer.
- Cost is generally related to use: the more you use a bureau, the more it costs.
- The time taken to do the work may not be tolerable in some cases.
- Time for on-line use may not always be available when you need it.
- You are limited to the services the bureau offers, and when it offers them.
- You must pay for phone charges if using on-line services.

This is not a fixed guide to bureaus; you may find that some bureaus have different charging policies, and are very flexible in their services. Don't forget to shop around.

8
EVALUATING SYSTEMS

THE HARDWARE

Processor

Only two major things are important as far as the processor is concerned.

- can it support the software you require?
- can it expand when you need it to?

Points to consider about processors:

- Remember that most small/medium size processors can support a maximum of 64K of RAM, unless specifically designed to take more, such as 96K or 128K.
- The maximum memory is not necessarily the amount that is available for use (*i.e.*, user memory); operating systems, etc., can use up quite a lot.
- Make sure there is enough user-memory to support your software.

- Is there memory expansion available? For example, if you have a 32K processor, can you upgrade to 64K? You may have to for some programs.
- How many types of interfaces can the processor support? (parallel, serial?) The more types, the more peripherals you can choose from.
- How many extra interfaces and peripherals can be added on?
- Are the interfaces industry-standard? If they are, you'll have a much wider choice of peripherals.
- How many programming languages does it have? If it has several, you'll have a wider choice of software available.
- If it's using floppy disks, can it take hard disks?
- If it's a standalone processor, can it be upgraded to multi-user? This option will depend on what your projected needs will be.
- Remember that the speed of the processor is in most cases not significant, since the speed of processing will depend on users, peripherals, etc.
- In some cases, the speed may be significant, particularly if coupled with fast, efficient language; for example, where there is not a lot of data entry, but a lot of complicated calculations.

VDU and Keyboard

The size, shape, and key layout of the keyboard will depend on the manufacturer, but watch for the following:

- All keyboards have the QWERTY layout.
- Keys must be large enough to allow easy use by the hand.
- Check the placement of the function keys: are they distinct from the text keys? In different colors?

- Check the placement of keys such as RESET or BREAK—they shouldn't be too close to the text keys.
- Pressure will vary from keyboard to keyboard: it shouldn't be hard or soft, although this is subjective.
- Sculptured keys are easiest to use, although not all keyboards have them.
- Check whether there are upper- and lower-case letters.
- Is there a separate numeric keypad? For much numerical work, this is useful.
- It's easier to have the keyboard separate from the screen.

As with keyboards, screens vary in size and style. The **configuration** of screen and keyboard, which makes up the VDU, may also vary.

- Screen integral with keyboard and processor.
- Screen and keyboard integral, separate from the processor.
- Screen separate, keyboard integrated with processor.

Whatever the configuration, make sure that:

- there is a brightness control;
- the screen is shielded from glare and reflection;
- the screen is not too high relative to the keyboard, and is not too far away from it.

Some other things to look for, but not always available:

- side-to-side swivel of the screen;
- up and down adjustable tilt.

When looking at the display (*i.e.*, the text or characters on the screen), make sure that:

- the text is crisp and clear, and not fuzzy around the edges, otherwise it will be difficult to read;
- the text is properly focussed, stable, and large enough;
- there is no divergence or skew; if there is, there are problems with the CRT.

The screen format will also be varied:

- you may come across 40, 64, 80, and even more columns across, by 18 or 24 lines;
- the choice of color or tint is up to you; most types are white on black, or green;
- if there is a lower case facility, are the descenders real ones (*i.e.*, appear below the line)?

If the screen is separate from the keyboard and processor, as distinct from a screen with a detachable keyboard, it will be either:

- a monitor, generally monochrome;
- a TV set, monochrome or color.

Finally, the best judge of the VDU and keyboard will be the person who is going to use it most.

Selecting Disks and Printers

With disk drives, you will often be limited to:

- what the processor manufacturer provides you with;
- what other manufacturer's equipment is compatible with your processor.

You can only choose disks if you have floppies:

- check with other people as to performance of the various brands;
- ask programmers too—they go through a lot of disks;
- there are many brands and prices around;
- don't buy disks from the manufacturer of the processor or the disk drive—they will be a lot more expensive;
- make sure the disks are compatible with the drives, as to sectoring, number of sides, and densities.

Generally, you will have a wide choice of printers, certainly with dot-matrix and daisywheels.

- Check that the printing densities and form widths are compatible with your requirements.
- If ribbons are used, see that they are readily available and easily replaceable.
- The power cords and connecting cables should be long enough.
- Make sure that the interfaces it can take match the one(s) you have, and that the baud rates are compatible.
- Ensure that any special stationery you may use will fit in the printer.

Documentation

Don't forget that you get documentation with all the hardware. It should be:

- complete, covering all aspects of operation, installation, repair, and maintenance;
- easily understood, with photos or diagrams of any special or tricky procedures;
- indexed and cross-referenced, preferably with summaries;

- the manufacturer's original documentation, not reproductions;
- applicable to the equipment, in terms of the edition.

The amount of the documentation you get will vary, but you must have manuals for:

- printer, disks, and other peripherals;
- processor—installation, repair, etc.

Optionally—if you want to do some programming—you will need:

- manuals on programming languages, operating systems, and so on;
- a reference manual on the processor.

THE SOFTWARE

Although there are some well-established standards and conventions for programming and analysis, there are no such standards by which you as a user can judge good software.

Remember that programs will not run on differing makes of processor, even though the same language is advertised.

The only exception is if processors use a standard operating system. Even here, you must make sure.

Consider software, both packaged and custom, from these points of view.

Presentation

- What do the reports, summaries, or other printouts look like? Are they neat and well presented?

- Is the information presented in manageable chunks—on screen or paper?
- How is the screen laid out? If the processor has them, is full use made of highlighting, half-tones, etc.?
- Are the directions and interrogations written in clear, unambiguous English?
- Presentation has to have class, logic, and continuity. If it doesn't, forget it.

Errors

It's vital that you examine the error recovery provisions, for both human and program errors:

- When asked for a letter input, enter a number, and vice-versa. Does it crash?
- If it's using floppy disks, don't put a disk in, or try one different to the expected. What is the message to you?
- Try to exceed the limits of the data. Can you do so?
- When it asks for a certain key to be pressed, press a different one. What happens?

Try to do all the stupid things you can think of. If the system won't let you, it's a good one. Errors can also be bugs, so look for these as well:

- Are the calculations correct?
- Is the right data being processed, and the right answers being given?
- Are there any spelling mistakes?

Go through as much of the system as possible; examine all the options, and test it with as much data as you can.

It is generally rare to find bugs in software, but it pays to check and make sure. It will also give you more confidence.

Documentation

- Look carefully at all the documentation that is supplied, as this is vital to the successful use of the system.
- Is it laid out neatly, with headings, page numbers, summaries, examples?
- Is there a summary of all the commands you have to use? Is there an index?
- Does it make sense when you read it?

No matter how good the system may be, if the documentation is poor, you will not be able to use it properly.

However, there are very few good manuals around. If you find a system that suits you, you may have to put up with a bad manual.

Don't Forget!

- Evaluate the security provisions of the system. Can you make copies of the various data disks? How much access is there to the data? What happens to the data if the system crashes?
- Make sure that the software fits into the available memory on your processor.
- Is the system upgradable to models of processors with greater memory, or hard disks? Although this may not be particularly important, it shows the thought that went into its design.
- Will there be future releases of the system? Do you receive them?

- Will you be told about any problems or bugs that have arisen, and will they be fixed?
- If applicable, will you receive updated versions when government legislation changes?
- Check out other people who are using the software. Are they satisfied with it?
- How many people are using the software? If a system is established, any problems that may have arisen have been taken care of.

Last but not least, make sure that the software does what you want it to! This may sound too obvious, but don't let salesmen impress you with irrelevancies.

THE SUPPLIER

You will have more to do with suppliers and their reps, be they software houses or dealers, than anyone else. Choose them carefully. Suppliers can provide you with the following services:

- sell one or more types of hardware;
- sell hardware and packaged software, either their own or of other manufacturers;
- write custom software for given hardware;
- any combination of the above.

First Impressions

- How long have they been in business?
- What is their background? Do they know what they are talking about?

- Are the staff helpful? Can they deal with queries without hesitation and fuss?
- How many staff are there? If there are two people who do everything, from programming to selling, trouble may arise. This is particularly true if more than one type of hardware is sold.
- If hardware is sold, what do their workshops look like? Are they clean and tidy?
- Are other makes of hardware, or other people, criticized? It is unprofessional to do so.

The Sales Pitch

Salesmen are usually trained people, having good product knowledge, as well as an ability to recognize certain reactions in people and act on them. They must also be able to extract an order from you. Whether they do or not depends on:

- how the presentation is set up—are prices and brochures at hand, and manuals on show?
- the appearance of the salesman, punctuality, and his interest in you as a customer;
- the quality of the demonstration: is it conducted smoothly and confidently, in simple and slow English?
- the salesmen's honesty: are the services of the company, and the features of the system, accurately represented?

The salesman must inspire in you trust. If he or she doesn't, or fails in some of the above areas, beware.

Tailor-made Software

- Examine the specifications (they must be detailed), and make lists of all changes, errors or omissions before agreeing to them.

- Make sure that your needs are analyzed by professionals. Don't pay them to learn about your needs, they should advise you.
- Check their documentation, who writes it, whether it is edited, and its content.
- Beware of man-day or man-hour type quotes; not all work can be measured this way.
- Check how much feedback they will give you. Will you get reports on the progress of your work? Will there be meetings to discuss your work?

Packages

- Depending on the supplier, a good range of packages should be available for demonstrations.
- Sufficiently detailed overviews or broadsheets should be available for every package.
- Same points as earlier mentioned regarding advice, feedback, documentation.

Hints and Tips

- Shop around, and see as many suppliers as you can before committing yourself.
- Ask about other clients, and check with them as to quality, reliability, delivery, etc.
- Get as much as possible in writing. This will avoid any misunderstandings.
- Don't sign anything until you are absolutely sure of what you will or will not be getting.
- Don't go to any foreign suppliers. Unless you are buying an off-the-shelf package with no modifications needed,

you will end up with more problems than any price difference could offset.

- Remember that profit margins on the smaller hardware are not high, so something will suffer.
- Try to be as knowledgeable and independent as you can.

AGREEMENTS

Tailor-made Software Contracts

When the specifications have been agreed on, it is usual to sign a software contract. The form of the contract will depend on the size of the job, but should include the following:

- The specifications should be attached separately.
- The terms of delivery should be stated.
- The method of costing, and an itemization of all costs, should be shown.
- The cost breakdown should include conditions on retentions, deposits, progress payments, and balances payable. It is unlikely you will pay for the whole system after it is completed; some form of deposit will have to be made.
- Variations: is this a "frozen contract" (*i.e.*, will you not be allowed to change anything)? If you can, you'll probably be charged for it.
- Warranties should be set out, as well as all the after-sales support. If there aren't any, find out why.
- The extent of training should be specified: how many staff will be trained, for how long, and by whom.
- Title to work done: this may be important. You should establish exactly who is the owner of the system, and what rights you or the software house have to further sales.

Hardware Contracts

A hardware contract can take the form of an order, a delivery statement, or a more formal contract. It should state:

- delivery times, and charges, if applicable;
- cost itemization, down payments, etc.;
- what is being bought, with serial numbers;
- what is not included in the purchase (*i.e.*, maintenance agreements, special accessories, etc.);
- warranties and replacement/repair policies.

Licenses

When buying a package, you should get a contract or a licensing agreement to sign.

- A licensing agreement means that the package is sold to you on a license, restricting your rights to copy and distribute it. It never really is yours.
- A contract should be signed for very large packages, and its form should be similar to contracts for tailor-made software.
- Check the position on replacement should the package have bugs, or if the disk wears out.
- Also check any obligations that may be placed on you, regarding use of the package.
- A maintenance fee is sometimes included in the license.

9

IMPLEMENTATION

INSTALLATION

Remember that the computer will work anywhere and under any conditions that you work in.

Location

- Keep the terminal away from background light, to minimize reflection on the screen.
- Ensure that there is enough light to see.
- Keep the contrast between the walls, tables, etc., and the screen to a minimum, if possible.
- Don't connect any equipment on the same power line as plant, large machinery, etc.
- Avoid locations with extremes of temperature and humidity, or with excessive dust.
- Make sure cables and power cords are not hanging loose, or in the way of feet.
- Keep equipment away from sources of noise.

- Ensure that the table, chair, keyboard, and screen are at a comfortable height.
- Make sure that there is plenty of room around the processor and work area.

TRAINING

Whether you get any training from your supplier will depend on:

- how you bought the system, hardware or software;
- size and type of system.

You generally won't get any training if you buy:

- a small, general-purpose off-the-shelf package;
- a small hardware system, with no software.

You will, and must, get training if you buy:

- a large, complex system, such as an accounting package;
- hardware and software together.

The number of staff trained, for how long, when, and where, will depend to a large extent on your supplier. The above points are all guidelines—some suppliers are willing to show you enough for you to get on with, even though it may not be required.

Training should cover all the following things:

- proper operation of all the hardware (turning on and off, cleaning, positioning, etc.);
- proper use of media (disks, loading paper, etc.);

- how to use any software;
- procedures—copying disks, care of media, error recovery.

USE

Before Switching On

Before you do anything with your computer:

- If transferring data to a computer, for example, ledger to disk, start with small batches. If you make a mistake, you only change a small quantity of data.
- Select a suitable time to transfer data—end of month for accounts, for example.
- Allow for plenty of mistakes to be made initially.
- Make as many mistakes as possible—with most you can't damage either hard or software, and it's a good way to learn.
- You must have parallel runs—processing data both manually and on computer, and compare results.
- If appropriate, get outside sources to verify the computer results,—*i.e.*, an auditor for accounts.
- If you need preprinted stationery, make sure that it is ordered and delivered in time.
- Remember that the keys on the keyboard may not have fixed functions, depending on your application.
- Don't get frustrated if you can't make sense of the manual. What you can't understand, try out.
- Make sure you use the computer a lot during the period of the warranty. Most of the physical problems should occur within this time.

Here are some day-to-day things to bear in mind when using the computer:

Care of Processor

- Don't use any solvents to clean any casings. There are suitable impregnated cloths available. In any case, follow the manufacturer's recommendations.
- Don't eat, drink, or smoke near the equipment.
- Don't bash the keys, or you'll get keyboard bounce, which will mean a new keyboard eventually.
- When the machine is not being used, put a hood over it. This will protect from dust settling on it.
- If moving the machine, make sure it is not connected to any of its peripherals.

Care of Disks

- ALWAYS keep floppies in their wallets. They are anti-static, as well as protecting disks from dust, etc.
- NEVER bend, fold, or otherwise manipulate the disk.
- NEVER touch any of the exposed areas of the disk. If you do, you'll lose everything on it.
- Don't leave disks too near TV sets, monitors, power cables, or any other source of magnetism.
- NEVER force a disk into its drive, or into the wallet.
- Don't stack disks in a vertical pile. Keep them upright, in a box.
- NEVER write on the disk's envelope. Write on a label first, then place the label on the disk.
- Make sure every disk is labelled correctly.
- Don't leave disks lying in the sun or near heaters or fridges, and keep them away from food, drink, and smoke.

Drives

- NEVER open the door of the disk drive if the drive is being used. You will almost certainly erase some data.

- Don't put anything except a disk into a drive.
- Disconnect the drives from the processor if you need to move either one.
- Follow the MANUFACTURER'S recommendations on cleaning heads, not what anyone else tells you.

Hard disks are less susceptible to misuse, but there are still a few things to watch:

- If using Winchesters, make sure that the drive is level.
- Don't break the hermetic seal. If you do, you'll probably need a new disk unit.
- Read the instructions for use carefully.

After Switching On

Remember that in most uses of the computer, entering data takes the form of a conversation between you and the program:

- the program requests data from you, by issuing messages or interrogations; it prompts you.

You then provide the program with data. What kinds of data?

- **numeric:** numbers, such as quantities, account numbers, prices, or dates;
- **monetary quantities**—often entered with a decimal point;
- **dates**—often entered with separators; for example, 28/10/83—the / is the separator;
- **responses to interrogations:** often a single character, such as Y for Yes, and N for No;
- **text:** names, addresses, letters, etc.

After the data has been entered, the program checks to see that the data is valid. For example, this entails checking:

- the type of data—numeric, special symbols, or text;
- the size or value limits of the data—for example, month not exceeding 12.

If the data is not valid for the given request, the program will usually ask you to enter it again, and the check is carried out anew. Sometimes, you may get a message telling you what you did wrong.

Numbers that are used in computers are classified into two types: integer and floating point. What type you use depends on what the program expects.

Integer

- An integer is a number that has no fractional part, and hence no decimal point—it is a whole number. Examples are 1, 59, − 110.
- An integer can be economically stored in the processor memory, and on other storage devices. However, there is a limit on the magnitude of the number. The smallest integer is 0.

Floating Point

- Floating point refers to the way numbers are represented in the processor. This representation includes a decimal point.
- Floating point numbers have fractional components, and hence decimal points. Examples are 1.0, 9.02365, −0.0008.
- Very large and very small numbers can be accommodated with this representation.

The most important difference between the two types of numbers as far as you're concerned is the presence of the decimal point.

PRESERVING YOUR INVESTMENT

Insurance

Computers and software are still quite expensive, and it pays to have adequate insurance coverage on both.

- If you are using them in an office, you could increase the value of the office equipment policy.
- In the home, they could be covered by home and contents-type policies.
- If your livelihood depends on it, see about loss-of-profits cover. If you have a lot of data stored, ask about recreation of records, should they be destroyed.

Maintenance Contracts

You may want to take out a maintenance contract, certainly on the larger machines, and if there is need, on the software as well.

If you have a small computer, a hardware contract may not be worth it. Warranty periods are becoming longer, and some manufacturers offer extended warranties for a nominal sum, probably less than for a maintenance agreement.

With hardware contracts, check the following:

- What services are provided, and at what times?
- Where are the services carried out—on site or at base?
- What are your obligations as a customer?
- What is the response time? *i.e.,* how long will they take to come and fix your problem?
- If it is a major problem, will you be given a replacement machine?

Average rates for maintenance are between 9% and 12% of the purchase price per year. Higher percentages may mean:

- hardware troubleprone;
- maintenance supplier charging too much.

With software, it may not pay you to have a software maintenance contract, unless:

- you have more than one large system;
- it processes a lot of data;
- the system and data are important.

If you have small packages, any problems that may arise may be fixed by the originator. Sometimes, the license fee may include maintenance.

In any case, shop around and get the best deal you can.

Security

Security as applied to computers may take two main forms:

- backups;
- unauthorized use.

To **backup** is to make copies of disks. If you have any disks with data on them, make sure you make copies. If you don't, and the disk fails, you will have to re-enter all the data!

Follow instructions for the given software, but make sure that:

- The program disk is copied; many software originators do not allow copying, and inhibit such provisions, to prevent piracy. If this is the case, you will need to buy a copy, at a nominal sum; some give you a copy with your package.

- The data disk(s) are copied.
- The originals are stored in a SAFE place.

Depending on the type of hardware and/or software, there may be provisions to allow only selected people to operate the system. These provisions may take the form of:

- **passwords**—group of characters that uniquely identifies the operator;
- **access levels**—codes that determine how much access the operator has to data.

If you have an installation with more than a couple of terminals, you will probably have security provisions.

IF SOMETHING GOES WRONG

Although computers and software are reliable, you'll probably get something going wrong at some time.

Hardware

Two common causes of breakdowns are:

- loose connections;
- blown chips.

Before suspecting anything:

- check fuses in the equipment;
- check the power cords and connecting cables;
- check your power supply;
- always consult the troubleshooting chart in your manual.

Also remember:

- DON'T start poking around inside the equipment unless you know what you are doing.
- Processing hardware generally does not deteriorate gradually—it just goes wrong.
- NEVER attempt to fix anything, unless you know exactly what to do.
- DON'T attempt to remove chips from boards unless you know how to do it. You'll also need IC pullers and inserters.
- Chips can't be repaired—they have to be replaced.

Another source of trouble is disks and disk drives. Several things may go wrong here.

There most common is called by various names: I/O ERROR, DISK ERROR, etc. Such errors occur if:

- the disk is not inserted properly;
- the drive door is opened, or ajar;
- the disk has not been initialized and/or formatted;
- the disk has been damaged in some way;
- the disk has dust or other particles on it;
- the disk cannot rotate freely in its envelope;
- data on the disk has been erased, or some of it is missing.

The above condition is sometimes called *corruption*. This may occur if:

- the disk has been exposed to a magnetic field;
- the read/write head hiccupped and wrote nonsense onto the disk;
- data was written to the disk, but the directory was not updated.

If a disk has been corrupted, there is usually little that can be done to recover data, and the only option may be to initialize it again, erasing all the data.

Before giving up the disk, open the drive door, and jiggle the disk—sometimes this aligns it a bit better inside the drive—and try again. Also test that there is freedom of movement in the disk envelope, by rotating the disk with your fingers through the hub, but be careful!

If nothing seems to work, get the copy of the disk, and use that.

With Winchesters, you will not be liable to most of the above problems, since the disk is sealed. You could get a head crash, where the flying head lands unexpectedly on the disk, but this is rare.

With both floppies and Winchesters, the disk drive could also be faulty:

- the read/write head could be dirty, or covered with oxide, which results from contact with the disk surface;
- the analog board and/or motor control could be faulty.

If it is the drive, DON'T try to fix it yourself!

With other peripherals, check that they are on-line (there will be some sort of indicator for this), and that the fuses haven't blown.

> Note: Don't forget the troubleshooting charts, which are in most peripherals' manuals.

Software

If something goes wrong with the software, it may be one of several things:

- a bug in the software;
- a malfunction in the hardware; or

- a temporary hiccup in the hardware, which may corrupt the software.

As appropriate to the software, you may try the following:

- use any recovery procedures your software may have;
- turn the hardware off, and try again from the start.

If everything works well, but you are getting wrong data coming out, it may be many things. Get in touch with your software supplier.

For both hardware and software, it is a good idea to keep a log of:

- data, time, and software;
- type of problem;
- what was fixed, and when.

GLOSSARIES

GLOSSARY OF TERMS

algorithm: The procedural steps, or flow of logic, for the solution of a specific problem.

alphanumeric: Used to describe a character that can be a numeral or a letter of the alphabet or a special symbol. An alphanumeric keyboard has letters, numbers, and special symbols.

analog (n): A physical representation of measurement. In a speedmeter, the needle or beam of light that indicates the speed is an analog of speed. In a computer the analog is an electrical signal.

applications software: Software for solving specific problems, or for specific applications, *e.g.*, an accounting package; *cf.*, **systems software.**

architecture: The interconnection and organization of internal circuitry in a microprocessor or computer.

assembly language: A language using mnemonics to represent machine code operations. A low-level language.

asynchronous: Mode of transmission that relies on start/stop bits to inform the processor when transmission is initiated and completed.

attributes: properties, characteristics, or features of a device.

backup (n): A copy or duplicate of a disk; **(v)** to copy or duplicate the contents of a disk on to another disk, or some other medium, such as tape.

batch: Work to be processed by a bureau collected into a single job.

baud: Unit of measurement of transmission speed, equivalent to bits per second in serial transmission.

binary (adj): Two. In binary arithmetic the two digits 0 and 1 are used.

board: Synonymous with **card**, although sometimes used for larger cards.

booting: The technique of running a preliminary program to make a computer ready to operate, usually on turning it on. The computer "picks itself up by its own bootstraps." Also called **bootstrapping.**

bug: An error or undesirable aspect in a program, which prevents a program from working correctly or at all.

bureau: A company that provides the services of a computer and expertise to people who haven't a computer, and charges the user.

bus: A path of wires along which data travels from one or more sources to one or more destinations.

byte: A group of binary digits, usually 8, considered as one unit.

card: A small printed circuit board containing electronic components.

character: An element of a set of symbols, such as a letter or number, or a special symbol such as « » ? / +.

character printer: A printer that prints a character at a time, rather than a line or a page.

chip: Colloquial name for integrated circuit, derived from the small piece of special material on which the integrated circuit is chemically formed.

code: A system where letters, numbers, and other symbols are arbitrarily assigned a meaning.

cold start: Restarting the computer by turning it off and then on again. All programs and data in memory are lost.

command: An instruction to the processor, usually keyed in.

compiler: A program that translates high-level computer language statements (source program), which are understood by people, into machine code (object program) that the processor can act on.

computer: A machine which accepts data, processes it, and supplies the results of the processing as a result of certain instructions. A collective noun describing the processor and I/O devices.

configuration: General term given to the arrangement of physical units within a system.

conversational operation: transmission of data between VDU and processor in which data travels one character at a time.

copy (v): To create a duplicate, to reproduce data, usually applied to disks. The contents of one disk are copied on to another disk.

courseware: Term given to software used for teaching purposes.

crash (n): Failure due to a software error or a hardware breakdown. **(v):** To crash.

cursor: A flashing or stationary rectangle or thin line of light, used to indicate where data is expected to be entered on a VDU.

daisywheel: A circular disk with protruding spokes, resembling a flower with petals. At the tip of each spoke is a character. Daisywheels are used on daisywheel printers: The wheel rotates until the required character is in position, and a hammer flies out and hits it, impacting the character on to paper.

data: The basic facts that can be processed, a character or symbol representing a value or state.

debug: The process of tracing and removing bugs from a program.

dedicated: Only used for one specified task or purpose. A typesetter is a dedicated computer.

default: A value that a program takes on in the absence of any values entered by the person using the program.

descender: The part of a letter that appears below a baseline; *e.g.*, q y p g j.

dialog: Interchange of information between program and user. The program gives prompt or messages, and the user responds by entering appropriate data.

digital: Referring to the use of digits, particularly binary digits within a computer. A description of equipment which operates in this manner.

direct access: Method of locating, reading, or writing data, particularly on disks. With this method you go straight to the data you want, wherever it is on the disk; *cf.*, **Sequential access.**

directory: An index to the data contained on a disk. Also called a CATALOG.

disk: A storage device consisting of a flat circular plate, made of plastic or aluminum, coated with a magnetizable material. The disk may be **exchangeable, fixed, floppy,** or **hard.**

disk drive: A device consisting of a motor and a read/write head which enables data to be stored on disks. The motor spins the disk while the read/write head moves over the surface of the disk, reading or writing data.

dot-matrix: Name given to a type of printer that prints characters as a set of fine dots within a grid of rows and columns, called a matrix.

drop: The distance between the top and bottom of a sheet of computer stationery, measured in inches or millimeters.

dumb: Description of a VDU which offers only the basic facilities of data entry, display and transmission; *cf.*, **Smart, Intelligent.**

duplex: Description of transmission in which data flows in both directions (*e.g.*, between processor and peripheral) and at the same time. Also called **Full-duplex;** *cf.*, **Half-duplex, Simplex.**

editing: The process of changing or correcting data before committing it to the processor.

element: A member of a set which itself cannot be further subdivided. Applied to files, in which data elements make up a **field.**

elite: A size of type in which each character is 1/12" wide; 12 characters are printed to the horizontal inch.

emulator: A device, usually a combination of hardware and software built into a peripheral, that makes the peripheral behave like another, different peripheral, of a different manufacturer, for example.

erase: The same as delete, but more often used when dealing with magnetic media.

exchangeable disk: A disk that can be removed from its controlling hardware and housing (disk drive). Using exchangeable disks means that more than one disk can be used to store data. Floppy disks are exchangeable; *cf.*, **Fixed disks.**

execute: To carry out the instructions in a program. A microprocessor executes a program by reading and acting on the instructions. Synonymous with **Run.**

fatal error: A term used to describe an error in a program which stops you going ahead with the program.

field: A subdivision of a record, itself a collection of related data elements.

file: A piece of work, or several pieces of work, collected together on a disk, and given a name or number.

firmware: Generic term for all software that is permanently stored in **ROM.**

fixed disk: A disk which cannot be removed from its controlling hardware or housing (disk drive). One disk is used to store all data. Winchesters are fixed disks; cf., **Exchangeable disks.**

flatbed: Type of **plotter** where the paper is held flat electrostatically against a table.

floppy disk: A disk made of flexible plastic, contained in a square rigid envelope, available in 5¼″ (133 mm) and 8″ (203 mm) sizes.

format: The layout, presentation, or arrangement of data, on a screen, file, or paper.

forms: Different kinds of computer paper used in computer applications.

font: A set of characters of a particular style and size.

graphic tablet: Device for entering data in a pictorial form. A picture is traced over the surface of the tablet using a stylus (pen). The tablet senses the position of the pen, and translates the position into X and Y coordinates, which are then processed.

graphics: Term describing the display of data in a pictorial form. Pictures on a screen are displayed using pixels, and on printers using fine dots.

half-duplex: Description of transmission in which data flows in both directions (*e.g.*, between processor and peripheral) but not at the same time; *cf.*, **Duplex, Simplex.**

hard copy: Term for any printouts that appear on paper.

hard disk: A disk which is made of rigid material, such as aluminum. Hard disks may be fixed or exchangeable, and common sizes are 5¼", 8", and 14" (355 mm).

hardware: All the components of a computer that can be seen and touched.

hardwired: Pertaining to a feature, property, or characteristic of a computer that is fixed by hardware, rather than software.

high-level: Term describing a computer language in which the statements are closer to human communication than to machine code. Usually high-level languages can be easily read and understood by people since they consist of pseudo-English statements. To be used by a processor, high-level statements must be translated into machine code.

impact printer: A printer that relies on mechanical force, such as a hammer striking, to transfer a character on to paper, in conjunction with a ribbon. Dot-matrix and daisywheel printers are impact printers.

initialization: The process whereby a disk is made ready for storing data.

input (n): The data or instructions that are entered into the processor for processing. **(v)** To enter data or instructions.

instructions: A group of symbols in the machine codes of a particular microprocessor, representing an elementary action which can be performed by a microprocessor.

integer: A number that does not have a fractional part or decimal point; a whole number.

intelligent: Description of VDU which has substantial editing, graphics, and transmission facilities; *cf.*, **Dumb, Smart.**

interactive: A way of using a computer in which the user holds a conversation/dialog with the computer.

interface (n): An electronic device which arranges data and controls the transmission of data between a processor and an I/O device. **(v)** To link a processor with another piece of equipment. *e.g.,* This computer can interface with a graphic tablet.

interpreter: A program that translates high-level computer language statements into machine code. The statements are translated every time the program is used, since the machine code is not retained. Not an efficient way of translating, but easy to use.

key: 1. A switch on a keyboard representing a character. 2. A field within a record in a file by which that file is ordered.

keypad: A small keyboard, with fewer keys. Keypads are used for more specific applications, such as a numeric keypad for entering numeric data.

kilobyte: 1024 bytes; abbreviated to K or Kb. It is the unit of measurement of memory.

language: A means of expressing or communicating instructions to a computer, according to an unambiguous set of rules.

load: To transfer data or a program from a storage device, such as a disk, to the processor's memory.

low-level: Term used to describe a computer language that is closer to the microprocessor than to human languages. Low-level languages cannot be easily read and understood by people.

machine code: Binary representation of the instructions of the microprocessor. Machine code can be immediately acted on by the microprocessor, without any further translation.

magtape: (Magnetic tape) A tape on which data can be stored.

mainframe: A large, fast and expensive computer, with disk capacities of several hundred M and a memory of several thousand K.

medium: Material, usually describing the one on which data is stored. Video-tape and floppy disks are media.

megabyte: 1,024,000 bytes (1000 kilobytes); abbreviated to M or Mb.

memory: A collection of ICs (integrated circuits) in which data is stored. Each binary digit is stored as an electrical signal within the IC. Memory is classified as read-only or read/write, and its size is measured in K (Kilobytes).

menu: A list of all the programs that can be used within a package, or a list of all the tasks that can be performed by a program. The menu is displayed on the screen, and a letter or number represents each option. The option is selected by pressing the appropriate key.

message operation: Transmission of data between VDU and processor in which a line of data is sent.

microcomputer: A small, inexpensive, desktop computer, which uses floppy disks or small Winchesters, with a maximum memory of about 128K.

microelectronics: Field of electronics concerned with design and manufacture of integrated circuits.

microprocessor: An integrated circuit that contains all the components to perform the basic data processing operations, all in one package. A microprocessor must be connected to memory and I/O devices before it can be used.

minicomputer: A larger and more powerful computer than a microcomputer, which uses large capacity hard disks, works at much greater speed and has several hundred K of memory.

mnemonic: A group of three or four characters representing a machine code instruction; mnemonics are easier to use than binary digits (literally a memory aid).

mode: The current method of operation, or the current state of a device; *e.g.*, output mode.

monitor: A screen used to display the data received from a processor, or data transmitted to the processor. A monitor does not have facilities to receive broadcast signals or process sound.

monospacing: Method of printing in which each character printed takes up the same amount of space horizontally, irrespective of the size of the character.

nonfatal error: An error in a program that does not substantially affect the progress of the program.

nonimpact printer: A device that does not rely on mechanical force to print data. Methods such as heat or electricity are used instead.

nonvolatile: Memory that retains its contents when power is turned off. ROM is nonvolatile.

number crunching: Traditionally, using a computer for large or complex computational tasks; now applied to any task involving numbers.

numeric: Pertaining to data that consists only of numbers, rather than letters and numbers.

object program: A program in machine code. The source program is translated by a compiler to make the object program.

off-line (adj): Not working in conjunction with a processor. (See next entry for example).

on-line (adj): Working in conjunction with a processor; *e.g.*, when a printer is being used to printout data from the processor it is on-line. If it is switched over to be used independently as a typewriter, it is off-line.

operating system: A program, part of the systems software, which enables the processor to perform the data processing and control functions.

output (n): The results of processing. Anything which the processor puts out. **(v)** To transfer data from the processor.

package: A ready-to-use, prewritten program or collection of programs, complete with all the instructions and other information needed to use it. Packages concentrate on applications from which many people will benefit, rather than only a few people; *e.g.*, a word-processing package; *cf.*, **Tailor-made**.

page: The contents of a full VDU screen.

page operation: Transmission of data between VDU and processor in which a whole screen of data is sent.

parallel: Method of transmitting data in which the bits travel down a number of parallel wires (usually 8, which is the size of a **byte**).

parity: Method of detecting errors in data transmission, by adding a bit to the byte being transmitted, and checking that the sum is the same after the transmission.

Pascal: High-level compiled computer language, not restricted to any particular application, named after the French 17th-century mathematician Blaise Pascal.

peripheral: A device which is not part of the processor, and contained in a separate box. I/O devices such as printers and disks are examples of peripherals.

pica: A size of type in which each character is " wide; 10 characters are printed to the horizontal inch.

pixel: *Picture cell* The subdivision of a scan line (see **Raster scan**) into many fine points, each called a pixel. Many thousands of pixels make up an image on a screen.

platen: In a printer, a metal plate or roller which forms a surface for the striking mechanism.

plotter: An output device which provides data in pictorial form. A pen controlled by two motors moves in the X and Y directions, drawing a picture which is defined in terms of X and Y coordinates.

port: An outlet in a processor where a peripheral plugs in, in equipment where the peripheral is compatible with the processor.

printer: A device that prints data received from a processor on to paper, using **Impact** or **Nonimpact** methods.

process (v): As applied to computers, to operate on data according to the instructions given for the job.

processor: The combination of memory and a microprocessor which is responsible for all operations on data that has been input, the subsequent output, and control peripherals. The processor needs an operating system in order to be used.

program (n): The set of instructions composed to make a computer perform specific activities, such as solving a problem. The instructions that are ultimately obeyed by the processor are numerical codes particular to the microprocessor. Often, programs are written using pseudo-English statements, which have to be translated. These pseudo-English statements make up the artificial programming or computer language. Writing programs is called programming. Also used as a verb.

prompt (v): To ask for data from someone using messages or interrogations—a program prompts you for an answer, for example; **(n)** the message or interrogation that asks for data.

proportional: Method of printing characters in which each character takes up only the horizontal space it needs, rather than a fixed amount of space; *e.g.*, the character *i* takes up less space than *m*.

random access: Referring to memories, both RAM and ROM, in which any bit may be accessed in the same time, no matter where it is physically located in the memory.

raster scan: Most common technique of displaying images on a screen, using the same principles as with a TV. The screen (the raster) is divided into many fine horizontal scan lines, which are in turn divided into pixels. The result is a grid of many thousands of points, and a picture is built up by the electron beam sweeping each line from top to bottom.

read: To transfer data from one storage device, such as a disk, to another, such as RAM. Data is read from a disk or memory.

read/write head: An electromagnet in a disk drive that reads data from and writes data to the surface of the disk.

record: A part of a file, itself consisting of fields; *q.v.*, **field, file, element.**

resolution: The ability to resolve, or distinguish two points, as applied to graphics devices. The higher the resolution of a device, the more points are used to define the picture, resulting in a better quality.

run (v): When a microprocessor carries out the instructions of a program, the program is said to run.

screen: The display surface of a CRT; the term is often applied to a VDU also.

scrolling: A screen can only display a limited amount of characters, less than can be stored in memory. To bring other data into view, a line of characters is removed from the top or bottom of the screen, and a new line brought in. This action is repeated continuously, giving the illusion of text moving past the screen, in the manner of a scroll.

second-user: Name given to secondhand, or used, computers or peripherals.

sector: A subdivision of a track on a disk, which is the smallest quantity of data that can be read or written by the processor. Typical sizes of sectors are 256 and 512 bytes.

selectable: Describing some feature or facility of a device which can be chosen by the person using the device from several other facilities present.

sequential access: Method of locating, reading, or writing data, particularly on a tape. All preceding data has to be gone through before the required data is reached. This is the way an ordinary music cassette works.

serial: Method of transmitting data in which the bits travel down one wire, one bit after another.

signal: A physical conveyor of data, such as voltage.

simplex: Method of sending data in which data flows in one direction only, *e.g.*, from the processor to peripheral; *cf.*, **Duplex, Half-duplex.**

smart: Description of a VDU that has some editing, graphics, and data transmission facilities; *cf.*, **Dumb, Intelligent.**

software: Term applied to all the programs that can be used on computers. Sometimes also includes the manuals and other documentation; *cf.*, **Hardware.**

sort (v): To order or arrange data in a particular sequence, according to a **key.**

source program: The series of high-level computer language statements that cannot be processed by the processor without translation into machine code.

sprocket holes: Equally spaced holes on both edges of continuous stationery for use by tractorfeed devices to feed paper through a printer.

standalone: Self-contained, not requiring any special add-ons or supports, *e.g.*, a standalone word-processor.

start/stop bit: Used only in asynchronous transmission, to describe one or two bits that are added to data to signify to the receiving device that data is about to be received, and that a timing device must be activated for the duration of the transmission.

stationery: Stationery is used to record results of processing using a printer or other device. Many printers use continuous forms fed through by sprocket holes at each edge. Several copies of each page can be obtained using multi-part stationery, with carbon paper interleaving.

suite: A group of related programs.

synchronous: Method of transmission in which only one central timing device synchronizes the sending and receiving. The processor and peripheral are always "locked" together.

syntax: The rules that govern the structure of language statements. The rules for writing the statements in a language correctly.

system: An interrelated collection of objects working together as a unit for a common purpose. A **computer** is a system.

systems software: A set of programs supplied by the manufacturer of the processor. Systems software comprises an operating system, a disk operating system if disks are used, and utilities.

tabulation: The facility of moving directly to a specific horizontal or vertical location on paper or on screen. The location itself is called a tab position.

tailor-made (also called **common**): Referring to a program or programs that are specially written for one particular task, for one set of people. Tailor-made software is usually commissioned by an individual customer, and not sold to anyone else; *cf.*, **Package.**

text: The words, numbers, and other symbols that make up data; *cf.*, **Graphics.**

throughput: A measure of the "productive work" done by a device. For example, throughput of a printer is the number of lines per minute it can print.

track: A division of a disk into concentric rings, like tracks of music on an LP.

tractor: A device on a printer that feeds paper through using two circular belts with protruding studs that catch the sprocket-holes on the edges of the paper.

transducer: A device that converts physical entities into an electrical counterpart. A microphone converts sound into electrical signals; a loudspeaker converts electrical signals into sound.

transmission: Transfer of data from one location to another, using electrical signals traveling along wires.

update: Generally applied to files, in which records are added, deleted, or amended, to ensure that the latest information is contained in the file.

utilities: Programs that are usually supplied by the processor manufacturer as part of the systems software. Utilities are not part of the operating system, but are used when needed, either on their own or within another program. Examples are the **Copy** utility and the **Sort** utility.

vector scan: Technique of displaying images on a screen, particularly suitable for precision drawings and animation. Vector scanning is only available on special VDUs. Images are created by moving the electron beam in the CRT to any place on the screen, just as a pen is moved in any direction on paper. The positions are specified as X and Y coordinates.

volatile: Memory that does not retain its contents when power is turned off. RAM is volatile.

warm start: Restarting the computer without turning it off and on again. Accomplished by means of a special key on the keyboard.

Winchester: Name of a type of hard disk. The disk is enclosed in a sealed unit, and a cushion of pressurized air supports the read/write head.

word: A unit of data, synonymous with byte.

write: To record on a storage device, such as RAM or a disk. Data is "written to" disk or memory.

user-friendly: Term used to describe hardware or software that is easy to use, by virtue of its design and the facilities offered to the user.

GLOSSARY OF ACRONYMS

A/D (**A**nalog-to-**D**igital **C**onverter): Device, usually an IC, that converts electrical signals into digital signals—those that only have two levels, and can be used by processors.

ADC The same as **A/D.**

ANSI (**A**merican **N**ational **S**tandards **I**nstitute): Body that publishes standards in computing and related fields, such as computer languages.

APL (**A** **P**rogramming **L**anguage): Highly-concise high-level programming language, originally developed as a shorthand for mathematicians, and subsequently implemented on computers. Requires a special keyboard with **APL** characters and symbols.

ASCII (**A**merican **S**tandard **C**ode of **I**nformation **I**nterchange): Universally used standard for representing characters as patterns of bits.

BASIC (**B**eginners **A**ll-purpose **S**ymbolic **I**nstruction **C**ode): Popular high-level interpreted computer language, not restricted to any specific applications, easy to learn and use, found on many small computers.

bit (**b**inary dig**it**): One of two digits that represent data in a form suitable for use by computers. All data can be reduced to binary digits.

CAD (**C**omputer-**A**ided **D**esign): Use of computer, particularly computer graphics, to assist in design.

CAI (**C**omputer-**A**ided **I**nstruction): Use of computer as teaching tool, not necessarily for computer studies.

CAL (**C**omputer-**A**ided **L**earning): Synonymous with **CAI.**

CAM (**C**omputer-**A**ided **M**anufacture): Use of computers as controlling or monitoring machines, for precision or high-speed manufacture.

COBOL (**CO**mmon **B**usiness **O**riented **L**anguage): Popular high-level compiled languge, restricted to commercial applications software.

CP/M (**C**ontrol **P**rogram/**M**icroprocessors): Widely used operating system on small computers.

CPI (**C**haracters **P**er **I**nch): Unit of measurement for printing density, being the number of characters that are printed in a horizontal inch.

CPL (**C**haracters **P**er **L**ine): Measurement of printing density or character spacing in a printer.

CPS (**C**haracters **P**er **S**econd): Unit of measurement for printing speed of printers.

CPU (**C**entral **P**rocessing **U**nit): Often-used acronym for a processor.

CR (**C**arriage **R**eturn): A key on a keyboard, often used when entering data into the processor. **CR** informs the processor when data entry is finished.

CRT (**C**athode **R**ay **T**ube): A tube in which a beam of electrons can be controlled and directed to produce a display on the screen.

CTRL (**C**on**TR**o**L**): A key on a keyboard that modifies the action of other keys to provide a shorthand way of issuing commands to a program.

D/A (**D**igital-to-**A**nalog Converter): A device, usually an IC, that converts digital signals (those on only two levels) into equivalent electrical signals, but ones that can be subsequently converted to a physical quantity. The analog signal does not consist of two levels.

DAC Synonymous with **D/A.**

DB (**D**ata **B**ase): A file of data which can access many different and independent programs.

DOS (**D**isk **O**perating **S**ystem): Program that is part of the systems software for a processor, responsible for all activities related to using a disk as a data storage device. May be called differently, but will usually have the **OS** ending.

DP (**D**ata **P**rocessing): Often used to describe all fields and areas of applications of computers. Using a computer is called data processing. There are also **DP** staff, departments, etc.

EIA (**E**lectronics **I**ndustries **A**ssociation): Organization responsible for several data transmission standards, a common one being the RS 232 for serial transmission.

EPROM (**E**rasable **P**rogrammable **R**ead-**O**nly **M**emory): A read-only memory that, once programmed, can be erased, usually by ultraviolet light.

FDX (**F**ull **D**uple**X**): Method of transmitting data to and from a processor or peripheral; data travels in both directions at the same time.

FORTRAN (**FOR**mula **TRAN**slation): Widely-used high-level compiled computer language, restricted to scientific and engineering applications.

GPIB (**G**eneral **P**urpose **I**nterface **B**us): An interface widely used in scientific or engineering measurement and control applications. Equivalent to IEEE 488.

HDX (**H**alf-**D**uple**X**): Method of transmitting data to and from a processor or peripheral; data travels in both directions, but not at the same time; *c.f.* **FDX**.

I/O (**I**nput/**O**utput): Describing all the activities of getting data in and out of the processor. Also describes peripherals that receive data from the processor, or transmit data to the processor. These are I/O devices. The term is not used as a verb.

IC (Integrated Circuit): A miniature electronic circuit in which all the components are chemically formed on a piece of special material. The piece is called a chip, and is packaged in a small rectangular plastic container.

IEEE (Institute of Electrical and Electronic Engineers).

IPS (Inches Per Second): Unit of measurement for the rate at which paper is fed through a printer. When printing is finished, it may be necessary to advance paper to the next page. The printer moves the paper quickly, and this movement, or slew, is measured in **IPS**.

K (Kb) (Kilobytes): Unit of measurement for memory storage; A **K** is 1024 bytes. If abbreviating to **Kb**, use a small **b**.

KSR (Keyboard Send/Receive): Description of printer that has a keyboard, enabling it to send data to the processor, as well as receiving data from it. An additional benefit is using the printer as a typewriter when not transmitting to the processor.

LF (Line Feed): In a printer, advancing the paper one printing line up. In a VDU, moving the cursor down to the next line on the screen.

LPM (Lines Per Minute): Unit of measurement of printing speed of a printer, or of its throughput. **LPM** depends on the number of characters in the line.

M (Mb) (Megabytes): Unit of measurement for memory or storage; A **M** is 1,024,000 (1024 × 1000) bytes.

MODEM (**MO**dulator/**DEM**odulator): A device installed between a processor and a telephone line to enable transmission of computer (digital) signals down telephone lines.

MS (milliseconds): One-thousandth of a second.

OEM (Original Equipment Manufacturer): In its most common use, the term describes a supplier of computer equipment who buys at discount large quantities of equipment from the manufacturer, places his own name on the equipment, and sells it to the user. **OEMs** are very common in the computer industry, and through them large quantities of equipment can be sold.

OS (Operating System): A program supplied by the manufacturer of a processor as part of the systems software. The **OS** makes the processor hardware work, and makes it as easy as possible to use the processor.

PCM (Plug-Compatible Manufacturer): Manufacturer of computer equipment whose products are compatible physically (plugs and sockets) and electronically (signal levels, transmission modes, etc.) with products of another manufacturer.

PROM (Programmable Read-Only Memory): Identical to a **ROM**, except that no data is written to it during manufacture—data can be stored in it when required by whoever uses it.

RAM (Random Access Memory): Memory that can store bits. Data can be written to **RAM**, and read from it. The contents disappear when power is turned off.

RO (Receive-Only): Description of printers that do not have a keyboard—they can only receive data from a processor; *cf.*, **KSR**.

ROM (Read-Only Memory): Memory that can store bits. Data can only be read from **ROM**. The original contents are written to it during its manufacture. Does not lose its contents when power is off.

VDU (Visual Display Unit): Device consisting of a keyboard and screen, used for receiving data from the processor, and for entering data into the processor.

INDEX

Acronyms, glossary, 127–31

Binary, 8
Bits, 8
Breakdowns:
  corruption, 110–11
  drives, 111
  errors, common, 110
  in hardware, 109–10
  log, keeping of, 112
  points to remember, 110
  software, 111–12
Bureaus, computer, 86–87
  batch, 86–87
    advantages, 87
    disadvantages, 87
  on-line, 87
Buses, 32–33
  S50, 33
  S100, 33
Bytes, 8

Characters:
  alphanumeric, 8
  ASCII, 8, 9
  numeric, 8
Chips:
  IC, 10
  microelectronic, 10
  wafers, 11
Compilers, 22
Computers:
  distinguishing features of, 1, 3
  measurement and control, 4
  number crunching, 3
  reasons for use, 3
  and software packages:
    education, 2
    games, 2
    housekeeping, 2
    memory size, 2
    professional, 2
  text processing, 4
  uniqueness, 3
Computers, types of:
  home, 75
  mainframes, 75
  micro, 74
  mini, 74–75
  power, 75
Custom systems. *See* Tailor-made systems
CRTs. *See* VDUs

Data:
  defined, 7
  entry pad, 63
  hierarchy of, 9, 10
  processing, nature, 7

Digits, 8
Disks, 53–58
  advantages, 53
  floppy:
    advantages, 57
    density, 55, 56
    diagram, 56
    disadvantages, 57
    sides, 55, 56
    typical, 56
  hard, 57–58
    advantages, 58
    disadvantages, 58
    typical, 58
    Winchester, 57
  sectors, 54
  specifications, 54–55
  storage on, 54
  tracks, 54
  types, 53

Evaluation, of systems:
  agreements:
    hardware contracts, 100
    licenses, 100
    tailor-made software, contracts for, 99
  disks, selection of, 91–92
  documentation, 92–93
  keyboards, 89, 90, 91
    configuration, 90
    format, 90
  printers, selection of, 92
  processors, 88–89
  software:
    documentation, 95
    errors, 94–95
    points to remember, 95–96
    presentation, 93–94
  supplier:
    first impression, 96–97
    packages, 98
    points to remember, 98–99
    sales pitch, 97
    tailor-made software, 97–98
  VDU, 89, 90–91

Financing, 83–86
  bank loan, 85
  hire-purchase, 85
  leasing, 84
  points to remember, 83–84
  purchase, 84
  rental, 85
  second-user, 86
  and software, 85

Graphic tablets, 62–63
  nature, 62
  use, 62, 63
Graphics:
  flatbed, 60
  motors, 60
  plotters, 60–62
  specifications, 60, 61

High-level language, disadvantages to, 23

Information, 7
Input, 6
Installation:
  disks, care of, 104–05
  drives, 105
  location, 101–02
  prior to use, 103
  processor, care of, 104
  training, 102–03
  use, discussion:
    checking, 106
    floating point numbers, 106
    integer numbers, 106
    programs, nature of, 105–06
Instructions to computer:
  programs, 17
  software, 17, 18
Insurance, 107
Interfaces: *See also* Peripherals
  standards for:
    EIA RS232, 31
    emulators, 31
    IEEE 488, 31

plug-compatible manufacturers, 31
translators, 31
types of:
Centronics, 32
General Purpose Interface Bus, 32
IEEE 488, 32
parallel, 32
RS 232 (V24), 32
serial, 32
Interpreters, 22

Jargon, 4–5

Keyboards, 41–44
carriage return, 43
control key, 43
data entry keys, 43
diagram, 42
function keys, 43
generation in, 41, 43
and processor, 44
QWERTY type, 43
softkeys, 44

Languages:
applications:
ANSI, standards of, 26
BASIC, 25
COBOL, 24
commerce, 24
education, 25–26
FORTRAN, 24
Pascal, 25
PILOT, 25
science, 24–25
for computer:
artificial, 18
elements of, 19
natural, 18
and processor, 19, 20
in programs, 18, 19
use, 19, 20
levels of:
assembly, 21
high-level, 21
low-level, 21
machine code, 20–21

Maintenance contracts, 107–08
Measurement and control, by computer:
digital/analog conversion, 67
analog/digital conversion, 67
thermostat, example, 68
Memory:
architectural, 13
EPROM, 15
erasure, 14, 15
and kilobytes, 13
nature, 13
PROM, 15
RAM, 14
ROM, 14
sizes, 13
Microprocessors:
distinguished from computer, 11
effects, 11
and input/output, 12
nature, 11
Modems, 58–60
acoustically coupled, 59
hardwired, 59
transmission, 59–60
use, 59

Needs, for computers, analysis of, 78–80
benefits, realization of, 79
computer, essentiality of, 79
costs, 80
points to remember, 78

Object program, 22
Output, 6

Packages, of programs, 82–83
Peripherals, 28–30
diagram, 29
and interfaces, 28, 30
nature, 28

Peripherals (continued)
and processor, 30
separate from processor, 30
use, 28
Plotters. *See* Graphics
Ports, 33
Printers, 44–52
characteristics, 44–45
feed:
press, 46
tractor, 46
high-volume, 52
impact, 45, 46–51
daisywheel, 48–49, 50
dot matrix, 46–48
spacing, 48
specifications, 47
jets, 52
line, 50–51
non-impact, 45, 51–52
electrosensitive, 51–52
thermal, 51
ribbons, 50
types, 50
Process, 6
Processing, 8, 9
Processors:
characteristics:
capacity, 16
design, 16
hardware, 12
nature, 12
periherals, 12
speed, 16
system, 12
word size, 16
Programming:
algorithms, 26
discussion, 26–27
elegant, 26
size of in memory, 23

Raster scanning, 64
advantage, 64
disadvantages, 65
pixels, 64

Security, 108–09
access levels, 109
backups, 108
passwords, 109
Signals, nature of, 7
Software:
and hardware, 81
language of, 76–77
points to remember, 81
sources, 82
for systems:
copy programs, 73
CP/M, 74
data in disks, 71, 72
disk operating systems, 71–72
disks, 72–73
direct access, 72
files, 72
firmware, 71
operating system, 70–71
sort programs, 73–74
utilities, 73–74
Source program, 22
Stationery, for printers, 52–53

Tailor-made systems, 83
Tape, magnetic, 65–66
access to, 66
advantages, 66
disadvantages, 66
use, 66
Terms, glossary, 113–27
Transmission, 33–36
asynchronous, 34
baud rate, 36
error checking, 35
full-duplex, 35
half-duplex, 35
modes, 35
nature, 33
parity, 35–36
simplex, 35
speed, 34
synchronous, 34

User-friendliness, 69–70
dialogs, 70
display, 70
error checking, 69–70
menus, 70

Vector scanning, 65
advantages, 65
disadvantages, 65
three-dimensional images, 65
Visual display units, 36–41
advantages, 37–38
and CRT, 37
cursors, 39
dumb, 40
editing functions, 39, 40
intelligent, 41
keyboard, 37
and monitors, 38
nature, 36
screen format, 39
smart, 40
specifications, 39
types, 38